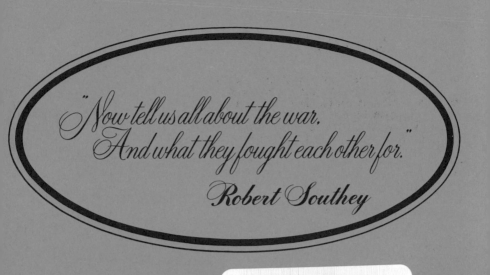

"Now tell us all about the war.
And what they fought each other for."

Robert Southey

The Battle of Fontenoy

Background Books for Wargamers and Modellers

The Battle of Fontenoy

Charles Grant

William Luscombe

First published in Great Britain by
WILLIAM LUSCOMBE PUBLISHER LIMITED
The Mitchell Beazley Group,
Artists House,
14–15 Manette Street,
London, W1V 5LB.
1975

© 1975 by Charles Grant

ISBN 0 86002 035 5

Photoset by Tradespools Ltd, Frome, Somerset
Printed in Great Britain by Tinling (1973) Ltd, Prescot, Merseyside

Contents

To Nell, of course

Illustrations

◇◆◇◆◇◆◇

Acknowledgements to Plates
The thanks of author and publisher are due to the following whose pictures are reproduced in this book: Plate 5 is reproduced by Gracious permission of Her Majesty the Queen; Plate 1: Les Archives photographiques d'Art et d'Histoire; Plate 3: National Portrait Gallery, London; Plate 8: National Army Museum.

Drawings by the author

Maps by Stephen Macphail

I
An Introduction
to Wargaming
❖❖❖❖❖❖❖

The proposition that the significance of an historical
battle can be more fully appreciated by those who have
participated in its re-enactment in miniature on a wargames table – a reconstitution in which representational
bodies of soldiery, possessing the fire power and
manoeuvrability of their life-size prototypes are
employed – is not so very unlikely. After all, consider
the professional methods whereby military problems of
all scales are solved, whether this is carried out on a sand
table at a military academy or through the complex
processes of a giant computer in the headquarters of a
super-power's strategic command. What we are considering is indeed no new thing, for the technique we
speak of – or something similar – has indeed been
practised in various forms throughout history.

However, in the context with which we, as practical or
potential wargamers, are more immediately concerned,
it initially flourished in the 19th Century, when much of
the planning of the Prussian, and later the German,
General Staff, on both tactical and strategic levels, was

carried out by means of the *Kriegsspiel* – the Wargame. It is in this particular aspect of the study of things military that we are especially interested. To avoid any possible misconception affecting our interests and aims, however, it must be made perfectly clear at this early stage just what our approach to the subject is to be. Now is the time to indicate that the operation in question is fundamentally a 'wargame', pointing out with some insistence, that the emphasis is on the 'game' portion of the word, rather than on the 'war' part.

It may, indeed, surprise the uninitiated to learn that the vast majority of wargamers are not professional military men (although it is far from unknown for soldiers, serving or retired, to be deeply involved in the hobby), and that their interest in, and their study of, the theory and practice of warfare in miniature stem largely from three distinct but closely associated causes. The first is fairly obvious – it is a basic interest in the history of all sorts of military operations, this being naturally bound up with the second, which is simply an appreciation of what an old and valued wargaming friend of mine described as the 'niceties of military millinery', or the evolution of the uniforms of the soldier throughout the ages. This particular facet of the wargamer's interest might be graced with the label of 'aesthetic', in that he is invariably eager to have the actual satisfaction of possessing and using accurately painted miniature figures in his battles, and to have the visual pleasure of arraying and manoeuvring them in colourful masses on his wargames table. Third, there is – and it is no means the least important – the active and very human competitive spirit which provides the impetus for players to wage quite innocuous war against their opponents, each attempting to confound the other by some sapient manoeuvre of his own. It must be reiterated, at the risk of being tedious, that what we are concerned with is wholly a game, albeit a serious one. This description in itself means that, while enjoyment of the game is paramount, it is nevertheless serious in that it should be a conscious and well-thought out attempt, based on a great deal of research and study, to recreate the conditions of warfare of yesteryear in the bloodless and amicable environment which provides the ideal framework for a wargame. It would be, I hasten to say, totally incorrect to claim that sweet harmony and brotherly affection are always present when such miniature battles take place. The human animal being the fallible and emotional creature that he is, as one fraught situation follows another and defeat – or victory – looms into sight, elation or despair can be seen writ large upon the customarily expressive countenances of the wargamers involved. It would then be unrealistic not to be aware of the hands, metaphorically and sometimes physically, rubbed gleefully together or to hear the occasional muttered objurgation escaping through tightly clenched teeth.

Such human failings to which wargamers are prone are not dwelt upon without reason. Experience – indeed many years of wargaming – has proved to me, with a very considerable number of games either fought or witnessed – that a player's temperament has a most significant bearing on his method of play and how he copes as a 'general' in miniature. To those unfamiliar with the wargame scene it must come as something of a shock to observe to what an extent the personality and character of an individual is reflected in his conduct as a wargamer; how the dashing and possibly even the irresponsible type will fling his armies and units about with the greatest élan and ebullience, taking all sorts of chances without fully considering their possible results, while he who is of a steadier and more phlegmatic disposition will carry out his manoeuvres with the greatest care and with the maximum attention to detail, refusing to take even the slightest risk which might redound to his disadvantage.

It may well seem odd that, in the harmless world of the wargame, the occasion will arise when the nerve of a player can fail him and he will shirk a decision which might put his fortune into the balance, even though it concerns the fate of but a score or so of miniature figures of metal or of plastic. Then, having failed, as it were, to seize the nettle danger, all too often he sees his plans and tactical combinations come to naught. It is far from our wish to suggest that the wargame is not so much an exciting pastime and a rewarding hobby as a happy hunting ground for the psychoanalyst, but one must witness a wargame to appreciate the tension that can be engendered in the older as well as the younger players – the dilated pupils and the flushed countenance (and note too that the wargamer glows not neither does he perspire) – the honest beads of sweat which are wont to trickle across the brow and to bedew the upper lip of him who is at grips with some fell enemy!

I dwell on this phase of wargaming activity not necessarily to show how excitable and frenetic players can be, but rather to make the very cogent point that with the participants becoming so bound up in what they are doing, there is a greater chance that, when an historical battle is refought as a wargame, much more will be dependent upon the human failings of the 'generals' and the proceedings will consequently have a far greater affinity with reality than would be the case were the game a purely mathematical one with those concerned being coolly objective in their approach to, and their analysis of, situations. In the frequently hectic and tense hurly-burly of a wargame the players relate much more to the generals of history, to Caesar, Alexander and Cromwell, who sat their horses in the very midst of action and were more affected by the din and tumult than were their successors of centuries later, ensconced in comfortable chairs in their war rooms, surrounded by maps and ministered to by orderlies and assistants. I do not think there can be much disagreement with the premise that it is very much more difficult to make a decision, right or wrong, in the heat and fury of a battle, to move a regiment from this or that quarter at a crucial moment, than to order an *aide de camp* to move a coloured block or a flag from one section of a map to another.

With all this in mind, it may be appropriate to repeat again the one salient point concerning what we are planning. This is simply that we are primarily concerned with a game which is, of course, something to be enjoyed by those taking part, and where the result for each of the several individuals participating is not necessarily so vital as it might be in other contests which might be more purely competitive. The true end product is the more complete understanding of the battle which has been refought, of the tactics used, and of the errors and miscalculations of the generals who were present. What we seek is a greater awareness of the problems these people in history faced and by attempting to reproduce them, even on a small scale, we hope to succeed in this laudable objective. The particular battle we shall be considering will be approached first of all from the point of view of the student of history. The events leading up to it will be summarised and considered, broadly from the political standpoint and, naturally, in rather greater detail from the military one. Every source will be closely examined in an endeavour to establish as accurate a picture of the course of the battle as possible, as well as to learn something of the character and capabilities of the generals or other important personages who either commanded in the field or who exercised some jurisdiction or influence over the combatant armies. To this will be added the fullest details relative to the actual fighting troops; their numbers and what particular qualities, if any, they possessed.

Obviously, of course, the weaponry, equipment and the tactics of the period with which we are concerned, must be explained and discussed, firstly so that the reader can be afforded a clear appreciation of the military institutions and 'mores' of the period. Equally as important, is the consideration that, when we restage the battle as a wargame, the rules we use and the capabilities of movement and firepower they reflect, will simulate as accurately as possible the actual conditions prevailing at the time with which we are concerned. One point there is which will not escape attention, is that the wargamers who take part as opposing 'generals' will, if they are at all worthy of their historical salt, have an enormous advantage over their long-dead prototypes, namely that of 'hindsight'. Each will therefore be keenly aware of the errors committed by their predecessors and will be anxious to avoid any of the pitfalls into which these individuals may have fallen. To obviate this is something of a problem, but one not wholly without solution. For instance, the 'battle' may be started at some point where the generals are largely committed to the broad framework of the historical setting, or indeed they may be given orders by the supervising authority which are in accord with the general theme of the battle and leave no room to make unreal decisions or to carry out manoeuvres not in the spirit of the period in question.

A not inconsiderable experience of such matters suggests to the writer that once the wargame is well under way the players lose no time in adopting the mantles of those generals whom they represent. The battle in consequence flows as naturally and fluidly as 'the real thing', irrespective of how many centuries in the past it took place. Once a decision has been reached – whether or not it repeats that of the original is no matter – then there is no doubt that the players will most certainly have learned much from what they have been about. Their understanding of the battle they have refought will be most assuredly far greater by reason of the experience than could have been derived from the cold print of a volume of history.

2
The Eighteenth Century

❖❖❖❖❖❖❖❖❖❖❖❖❖❖❖❖❖

To the military historian and student there are few epochs which provide such a wealth of fascinating material for examination as does the 18th Century. In it the wargamer can discover, as the decades unfold before his eager gaze, the most diverse of battles of all kinds, ranging from the skirmish and the ambuscade, through the gamut of many varying sorts of formal battles to escalades and prolonged formal sieges, each and every one ready for adaption and re-enactment. The early years of this most colourful century saw the art of war dominated by the great Duke of Marlborough – arguably the greatest British commander of all time – and those illustrious contemporaries, his great colla-borator Prince Eugene, the Marshal Duke of Berwick, and such French generals as Vendôme and Villars. Armies then had but recently changed from the ponder-ous bodies of musketeers and pikemen that had tramped laboriously about the stricken fields of Britain and Europe during the English Civil War and the Thirty Years War, the two characteristic struggles of the previous century.

In the middle years of the 18th Century came the lengthy series of wars which racked the Continent, spreading ultimately to far-off India and across the Atlantic to America and Canada. The great names then were Frederick the Great and Maurice de Saxe, and to a lesser extent such as Frederick of Brunswick and Wolfe of Quebec. The century ended with the War of American Independence, and at the same time saw the beginning of the great wave of fiercely nationalistic and partisan armies which characterise the French Revolutionary and early Napoleonic Wars.

Although on the surface the century seems to have furnished little that was militarily new (tactics being based throughout the period on the smoothbore musket and cannon), it did provide some significant changes at least in concept. The contrast between the plug-in bayonet, just becoming obsolete with Marlborough, and the Baker Rifle and Congreve Rocket – the shape of things to come – shows quite dramatically just what changes were in fact taking place. Between the two extremes we find a steadily formative period wherein, although military professionalism was complete, and where consequently one might expect to discover total conservatism, there was a tremendous quickening of thought. This, it has to be acknowledged, was not confined to military circles only, being notably present in political and other spheres, and men everywhere were bringing forth fresh ideas and new concepts to influence and to rock the very fabric of society and its institutions.

Thus, largely due to the experience of generals who had commanded troops in the field – and some indeed were far-seeing individuals – as well as to the considerable body of civilian scientific thinkers, military technology and practice were coming under severe appraisal and criticism for obsolete methods and outworn traditions. The names of the Frenchmen, Gribeauval, La Vallière and Guibert are notable in 18th Century military history as being pioneers in the streamlining – if we may employ a modern term – of contemporary military institutions. Their ideas and innovations were to have long standing success into and even beyond the Napoleonic era. Throughout military Europe there was an overhauling of established military practices and much was done – not always wisely, it must be confessed – to bring about a 'new look' in many national armies. A multitude of inventions and innovations were also available for the more enlightened military minds to consider. Nor was there a lack of opportunity for such ideas to be tried in the crucible of war, for two major conflicts, the War of the Austrian Succession and the Seven Years War, filled the middle years of the century, following so closely on each other that they provided an almost continuous period of warfare. Thus, new methods and innovations could be readily put to the most practical of tests, the exigences of active service.

It is indeed from these three decades – roughly 1740 to 1770 – that there comes some of the most interesting and varied military achievements and enterprises. What is especially noteworthy is that, in a rather strange fashion, warlike activity was undertaken by the military with a complete disregard for the civilian population resident in the area where operations were taking place. By this it is not meant that civilians were treated cruelly or even with undue harshness but simply that their existence was more or less ignored. *Per contra* – it must be said that this was also the attitude of the non-military to the troops they saw continually passing to and fro in their midst. At this stage, it is hardly necessary to point out that there was absolutely no cause whereby the minds of the people could be inflamed – or if there were, there was as yet no demagogue ready to rouse them from their political and social apathy, although many such would not be long in appearing. Social position was largely predestined and generally accepted.

Thus, as a general rule, people and their property were fairly well respected by the soldiery, this being in the greatest possible contrast to the days of about a century previously, when during the great religious wars, people of every class, peasantry and bourgoisie alike, had been subjected to the most dreadful treatment by troops of the opposite religious persuasion. Massacres, looting and rapine were then commonplace, and an acute degree of privation was the norm of everyday life in many parts of Central Europe. In the rather more enlightened days of the 18th Century – the beginning, indeed, of the Age of Reason – although doubtless there was the occasional outrage (it would be ingenuous to suppose otherwise, especially where less disciplined troops such as those recruited in great numbers from the Balkans by Austria were concerned), the general behaviour of soldiers towards the civilian populace could have been a great deal worse.

Despite the increasing awareness of the importance of the individual in society, it must be admitted that this moderation was due mainly to the military system which prevailed at the time. Armies in the field continued to move with considerable deliberation, and to avoid the uncertainty of local requisitioning of supplies, they were largely based on fortresses where stores of food and munitions could be accumulated during the winter months preparatory to the normal summer campaigning season. Despite the existence of such 'magazines', armies were ordinarily accompanied everywhere by great baggage trains, thus cutting down the foraging and the 'living on the country' which so distressed French generals in later Napoleonic times. Obviously, with his needs more or less catered for by the wagon train, there was much less likelihood that the soldier would go off on a looting expedition, to the detriment of his military duties, as well as possibly goading the populace into taking reprisals.

In this fashion then, people as a whole did not involve themselves in the messy and inconvenient business of making war, and it was left almost entirely to professional generals and their troops, whose livelihood it was. Thus, one result was an almost complete absence of any desire to wage war *à l'outrance*, that is to say, without limitation of time or objective, the aim being the complete and immediate destruction of an enemy. Firstly, to achieve this objective was a bloody business entailing, even in the event of an unqualified success, heavy losses in men and material by the victor, thus inevitably incurring – as was ever the case – the country's disapproval of its general's actions. The reaction and indeed the revulsion to the losses incurred by Marlborough's army at the Battle of Malplaquet is a case in point.

Secondly, and equally important, was the fact that a complete victory would have left no one against whom a victorious army could be employed, this resulting in wholesale demobilisation of the troops and subsequent unemployment of the generals who had led them. Sadly but truly, therefore, it has to be pointed out that, in the era with which we are concerned, it was to the advantage of many commanders to keep a war going, and many were no doubt guilty of just that. Again, one has to think of Marlborough, for the Duke had many detractors ready and willing to point out the not inconsiderable pecuniary advantage he enjoyed as a military leader, and the colossal military and political power accruing to him during the long years of the War of the Spanish Succession.

Thus, for a variety of reasons, what we have come to understand as 'total war' – with the complete political destruction and military overthrow of an enemy as its aim – was inconceivable in 18th Century terms, and limited objectives were very much the order of the day. Inevitably then, warfare developed many of the characteristics of the game of chess – movement and tactics became highly formalised, exact values were placed upon specific objectives and in every respect the manoeuvres of armies resembled quite distinctly the movements of pieces upon a board.

Fortresses, upon which armies were based, became more important targets than the armies themselves and much of the technique of warfare was devoted to neutralising or capturing them, the latter usually by formal siege operations, for to make a direct assault was suicidal in the extreme. Such fortresses were, indeed, something more than mere towns surrounded by a wall, and two great names stand out in the history of these strongholds – Vauban, a Frenchman, and Cohorn, who was Dutch. The walls they built were planned and constructed with mathematical precision so that no single section could be attacked by an enemy without flanking fire being poured destructively upon him. To reach the walls, indeed, the attackers had to cross a deep and wide ditch and mount a 'glacis' – a smoothly sloping area commanded by fire from the walls. These latter, as well as turrets and bastions, were liberally garnished with heavy guns, and it can readily be seen that an all-out attack upon such a defensive structure was something to be considered most carefully by any commander.

Long term blockades were therefore the order of the day, initially, at least, in the hope that privation and lack of food would cause the defenders to lose heart and capitulate. Formal sieges were assisted by great batteries of artillery whose fire would be concentrated on a chosen section of the wall over days and often weeks, until a sufficiently wide breach had been made to give the attackers the opportunity of a direct assault. This species of operation was conducted with the greatest attention to details of technique and protocol, and the duration of time which any fortress could properly be expected to hold out was most delicately calculated. It was no disgrace for a fortress commander to surrender once siege operations had advanced to a point where experience showed that an assault, if launched, could succeed. Woe betide him, however, were he to be stubborn enough to resist a little too long and to give the unfortunate people of the city he was defending up to the horrors attendant upon a successful storm. Such an occurrence – and indeed any sort of major clash – would be a bloody business. Despite the conventions of the 18th Century, fighting resulted in very high casualties more often than not, this being very apparent because of the rudimentary state of medical science at the time. In the field any severe injury to a limb necessitated instant and complete amputation, and abdominal wounds often meant certain death. Gangrene, and the shock resulting from amputations crudely carried out, resulted in an enormous number of fatalities; certainly as many died in hospitals as did on the actual battlefield itself. Warfare, even in the Age of Reason, was a very unpleasant thing.

However, as we have indicated, a great portion of the campaigning season – and this was generally summer alone – was taken up by complicated manoeuvring, marching and countermarching as the opposing armies jockeyed for some advantageous position whereby the enemy could be forced into beating a retreat without unnecessary risks having to be taken.

This coming and going was a very deliberate business and with the fighting men accompanied by the great baggage trains of which we have spoken, a prodigious 'tail' was created which was very open to enemy attack. It is in connection with this that we briefly note the first real break with the old tradition of the ponderous armies of earlier days, this phenomenon being the appearance of light troops, both horse and foot. The relative immobility of the baggage trains resulted in their being open to sudden raids and incursions by swift moving units. Their vulnerability to this sort of operation becomes obvious, and to defend them, other light regiments had to be employed. Thus, in every quarter where armies operated in the field such soldiers were raised and recruited. They were by any standard a polyglot agglomeration of semi-regulars and other types, without any species of formal organisation and doubtless including a substantial leavening of ordinary down-to-earth brigands, many emanating from the less civilised portions of the countries involved in the war being fought at the time. Austria had a particularly large population of such types, from which she could draw large numbers of recruits, the Balkans providing a wealth of the most colourful types – Pandours, Tolpatches and Croats, while from Hungary came the archetypal light cavalryman, the *hussar* – not to be confused with the later Napoleonic military dandy, but a much more primitive individual whose outlandish appearance was frequently sufficient in itself to fill a foe with the liveliest apprehension. Russia of course had similar troops – the Cossacks – while France raised an astonishingly diverse selection of units, some bad, some mediocre but some exceedingly skilled in their specialist role: the carrying out of ambushes, raids and reconnaissance, the last especially being the one in which they were most frequently used.

Fig. 1. Officer, Arquebussiers de Grassins (French)

One notable individual in this connection was a certain Fischer, a one-time body servant or valet, whose *Chasseurs*, both horse and foot, performed remarkably well in the 'petite guerre' for which they were developed.

The nomenclature of other units in the French service was quite resounding, these including the *Arquebussiers de Grassin*, the *Fusiliers de la Morliere* and the *Fusiliers de la Montagne*. Their uniforms were as varied as their names and origins, but they were in fact the precursors of the highly-trained light infantry of the years to come. Such corps as the famous Light Division of Peninsular days were naturally as yet undreamed of, but much of the great Sir John Moore's system of training stems from the methods of his less sophisticated predecessors.

Frederick the Great of Prussia, whose name must surely be included in any list of Great Captains and who was one of the dominant military figures of the 18th Century, was rather more conservative. This was possibly understandable, for at a time when discipline was truly ferocious, above all in the Prussian service, the King did not look kindly upon troops whose function took them for long periods far away from normal supervision. Desertion was a thing always to be feared, and such expeditions gave an ideal opportunity for the disaffected to vanish. Nevertheless, Frederick did have numbers of *jäger* battalions, both *zu fuss* and *zu pferde*, and also a most useful light cavalry, mainly hussars of Polish origin, whose doyen was the celebrated Von Ziethen.

Britain, however, lagged behind and her armies were singularly deficient in any sort of light infantry or cavalry, although the raising of Highland regiments with a tradition of mobility and independence of action did provide the nucleus of a corps of light infantry until the War of American Independence, when several catastrophes to British arms pointed out dramatically the disadvantages a formally drawn-up army suffered from when not provided with a screen of light troops. Such troops were not of course expected to take their place in the line of battle, but normally covered the flanks and the rear of armies.

By the fifth decade of the 18th Century the artillery arm had still not realised its full potential, but the succeeding few years were to see the beginning of something like a revolution in both tactics and material. In the time of Marlborough the gunners had been semi-professional while the gun teams and their drivers were drawn largely from the civilian population, being hired for a period. However, by the year with which we are concerned, regular artillery regiments had been created in the majority of armies and some improvements had been carried out in the mechanics of moving the guns from place to place, while drivers as well as gunners were soldiers. The combination of the weight of the ordnance in use and the fact that the gunners were all dismounted made artillery a pretty slow-moving force. The difficulties of getting guns about on a field of battle where there were no metalled roads, or indeed any worth speaking of at all, made it certain that once guns were placed in their battery positions at the outset of a battle, there they had to stay, unless of course they were of extremely small calibre.

Already, however, Frederick the Great was experimenting with a kind of horse artillery where the gunners, instead of being on foot, were mounted, thus enabling the guns – in theory at least – to move at something approaching cavalry speed, thus giving a 'punch' to mobile columns. Such innovations may seem to us to be elementary, but at the time they were rather startling. However, it is true to say that really mobile horse artillery did not come into its own before the later Royal Horse Artillery and the French *Artillerie à Cheval*.

In matters theoretical, too, things were moving along the right lines and considerable progress was being made towards the greater standardisation of gun calibres and a reduction of their number. The Frenchmen La Vallière and Gribeauval were two of the foremost artillery theorists of the time. Generally speaking, therefore, artillery techniques were superior to those of half a century earlier, although much still remained to be done.

Briefly, then, we have made a general appreciation of the military situation of the seventeen-forties and we have seen that warfare was conducted along very traditional lines. Although battles were still very deliberate affairs, they could, however, be more fluid than they had been only a few years earlier. It should be carefully noted that, strangely enough – and this may come as something of a surprise for the present day reader – men made war with considerable regard to a proper code of conduct. Certainly in one major aspect 18th Century conflict was far more humane than the behaviour we have come to expect in the present century – in the rapid exchange of prisoners. This was *de rigeur* for all ranks, not only officers, and unfortunate captives could expect to be released at the end of the summer campaigning season without, as happened in later wars, having to languish for years in prison camps.

With all the above in mind and armed, it is hoped, with an overall picture of 18th Century warfare, it remains for us to turn from the general to the particular.

3
Weapons and Tactics

❖❖❖❖❖❖❖❖❖❖❖❖

There is little need to stress the point that an examination of the various types of weapons – and their capabilities – with which the soldiers of any period were equipped, is essential to an understanding of the battles in which they fought. This is particularly important in any consideration of the art of war in the middle years of the 18th Century, in connection with which there exists many misconceptions regarding the manner in which troops operated, as well as the quality and effectiveness of the tools of their trade. The century-and-a-half which began with the era of Marlborough and ended with the Crimean War and the American Civil War can be described in general terms as the 'horse and musket' period, for it was the employment of these two factors which most materially characterised the warfare of the years in question. As time passed, however, the former (horse and, of course, rider) had become an increasingly less potent force on the battlefield, but of this more later.

The great bulk of infantrymen who took their place in the line of battle were armed, whatever their nationality, in an identical manner – with a heavy, smooth-bore musket, a bayonet and possibly a short sword, or hanger. To be accurate, the last named was little employed in a strictly military sense, being more often brought into action as an entrenching device or a cooking utensil, on which could be impaled a piece of meat preparatory to its being held over the flames of a camp fire. It is important to note, too, that the other feature of the period, the horse, was far from being the highly bred and fast racing or hunter type animal, but was, in fact, heavy, slow and totally incapable of proceeding – especially when one considers the weight of rider, arms and equipment that was carried – at much more than a canter, with a deliberate sort of gallop as the maximum gait, and this only for short periods. There is also really a third element of the art of war in the 18th Century to be considered – the cannon. This was, again, a smooth-bore weapon which, possibly to an even greater degree, subscribed to the vices and deficiences of its smaller brother, the musket.

The tactics of troops operating in the field must always conform to, and indeed are governed by, the available weaponry, and this is especially notable in the period with which we are concerned. It is therefore most essential to examine with some care the weapon which was most instrumental in dictating these tactics. This of course was the musket – in the case of the British Army that weapon which posterity has come to know as 'Brown Bess', and which altered only in the slightest degree during the very many years it was carried by British soldiers in every sort of clime and condition. While in some respects an admirable weapon, it had many defects – in modern eyes the most important by far being its quite staggering inaccuracy and the consequently extremely limited range at which it could be fired with effect.

During its long life 'Brown Bess' was subjected to all manner of tests by military authorities and other researchers. Without going into a great deal of detail, we find that the overall results were astonishing to say the least. They basically indicated that, to fire at any specific object at a distance of a hundred yards or more was virtually useless, and that a single man could stand with impunity at this range without even a trained and expert marksman's having a great deal of chance of hitting him, even with a fixed musket. At first sight, too, the loading procedure of the weapon was a complicated one, with a small amount of powder from a paper cartridge being poured into the firing pan of the musket, the remainder then being decanted into the barrel, followed by the wad – provided by the paper of the cartridge itself – and then the musket ball rammed well and truly home. When the trigger was pulled, the powder in the pan was ignited by a spark from a flint striker, the flame passing through the touch hole to explode the charge in the barrel, driving forth the ball – in weight a formidable leaden sphere of just under an ounce – on a somewhat erratic course. Misfires were fairly frequent, the use of poor quality powder rapidly 'fouled' the barrel, and flints wore out speedily. In action, there was general satisfaction if there was no more than one misfire in six rounds discharged.

Thus, with a short-range, very inaccurate missile weapon which threw a heavy ball – one has but to look into the barrel of a flintlock musket of the period to appreciate its massive size – tactics for infantry of the line were determined in advance. It must be remembered that, although the process of loading and firing the musket does appear to be a laborious and slow business, such was really not the case, for trained regular infantry could be expected to load and fire certainly three times a minute and, when pressed, possibly four times, this being the case with the infantry of Frederick the Great of Prussia whose highly disciplined blue-coats were trained to fire every sixteen seconds. Naturally, this rate could not be maintained for long, fatigue very quickly slowing down the speed of the operation. Nor indeed would it have been a good thing to use up the rounds carried in the ammunition pouch so quickly. What was carried in the way of ammunition by each man was insufficient to permit lengthy periods of rapid fire of this nature. Quick replenishment quite beyond the capabilities of the supply services would have been necessary.

What we have, then, are armies largely composed of infantry, armed with a highly inaccurate short-range weapon capable of rapid fire for a short period. From what has already been said of the musket it will be

Fig. 2. Private, infantry of the line (British)

obvious that there was no question of one individual's drawing a bead upon another with any hope of hitting him – except possibly at point-blank range. The tactics resulting from this fact simply involved a unit's – battalion, company or whatever – getting as close to the enemy as was practicable and pouring in as hot a fire as it could.

Naturally, individuals in such a unit had to be more or less shoulder to shoulder so that maximum density of musket balls in a volley could be achieved, and equally as naturally, the resulting closely-packed bodies made splendid targets for the fire from any enemy within range. For example, a white-clad French regiment would march up towards a red-clad British one and, using whichever system of firing was in favour – either by ranks or by small, tactical units such as platoons – deliver as heavy a fire as it could into the enemy ranks. The British would reciprocate in kind, both sides with the idea of inflicting an unendurable number of casualties upon the other and thereby forcing him to break and run by reason of the sheer weight of lead being received.

Accordingly, it was to a general's advantage to allow an enemy to approach to close quarters before opening fire. It has to be pointed out, however, that it was said that Frederick the Great ordered his men to fire at up to a range of three hundred yards, with the aim of simply frightening the enemy by the tremendous sound of the discharge. This may have succeeded with poor quality opposition, but it was ineffective against really good infantry and usually it was a case of waiting until one could see the 'whites of the eyes'.

There are, in fact, many references to the devastating results of such close range musketry during the period of which we speak. The volley delivered by Wolfe's infantry on the Heights of Abraham (1759) comes to mind. On this occasion the British general waited until the advancing French were no more than 30 yards away before ordering a single tremendous discharge which laid the enemy line in ruins. There is yet another instance with which we are more particularly concerned and which will be occupying our attention in due course.

Thus far, then, we have briefly described the nature of line infantry and considered its principal weapon. Light infantry was still in its infancy, its tactics usually rudimentary and, although the earliest types of rifle were to be found here and there, they were comparatively few in number. Light infantry was more often than not armed with the ordinary infantry weapons. As a species of specialist force its advantage was that, its recruits being drawn as far as possible from men accustomed to a country sort of life – foresters, hunters and so forth – they could be expected to have some kind of innate ability to act in a more individual and independent manner than was compatible with the training and discipline of line infantry. Hence we find them operating as a screen to the main body of an army, harassing and 'needling' the enemy, although frequently much of their activity was confined to operations against their opposite numbers of the enemy side. It was in raids, 'ambuscades' and similar enterprises that they came into their own.

In support of the infantry, and in a line of battle usually arrayed on the flanks or wings, was the cavalry, which, in the British army consisted of regiments of 'Horse' and dragoons. We must be quite sure that when we think of mounted troops we have a correct picture of what they were and how they fought, for the time when heavy cavalry could be expected to charge and overthrow unbroken and steady infantry had really passed and, as we have noted, the volume of fire that professional soldiers could produce was very considerable, sufficient save in the most exceptional of cases, to prevent a frontal charge by cavalry on the three deep infantry line which was the common deployment.

Having mentioned the cavalry charge it might be as well to indicate what we mean by the phrase, and to do this we are obliged to look at the animal concerned and the load he carried. By any standards this was a prodigious burden. Regiments of horse, and – possibly to a lesser degree – their counterparts in the French service, the *regiments de cavalerie* or the *cuirassiers*, were big men and consequently their mounts had to be correspondingly large and powerful, for the weight of arms, uniform, saddlery and other equipment was immense. Bearing all this in mind, it behoves us at the outset to dispense with any preconception that a cavalry 'charge' was the whirlwind thing of our youthful imagination. It was, at the optimum, carried out at a 'fair, round trot' only, and furthermore, it must be stressed that it was not possible to carry out a cavalry charge pressed directly home against infantry of any sort of quality. Thus, in formal battles, cavalry – usually numbering according to circumstance up to about a quarter of the entire strength of the army – would be found skirmishing with their opposite numbers, engaging in charge and countercharge, these usually consisting of riding fiercely up to

Fig. 3. Officer,
Gendarmerie d'Elite,
Maison du Roi
(French)

an enemy and backing away again without actually crossing swords. It was good tactics, of course, to act in this manner against infantry with the aim of, for instance, temporarily at least halting some advance, because, although there was no question of the cavalry's charging home, the infantry nevertheless had to halt and take up defensive positions when faced with such a threat.

Thus, we see that the function of heavy cavalry was really to protect the flanks of an army and against infantry it would be unleashed only when they were already badly shaken by musketry or artillery fire, or were in retreat or in flight. These were really the only times when it could be used with effect, and it was then that 18th Century heavy cavalry really came into its own. When hitting disorganised or unprepared troops the effect could be annihilating, the classic example being at the Battle of Rossbach (1757) when Frederick the Great's cavalry, executing a march behind a hill, mounted it and charged down upon long columns of French infantry who, totally surprised, were unable to form a front to counter the assault and were swept away.

In addition to the heavy cavalry of the line there were here and there in continental armies, units of light, sometimes irregular, horse. They were frequently raised in the less civilised portions of the territories of the warring powers and did not form part of the line of battle, being used for forays, raids and so on. One must also note another sort of cavalryman, the dragoon. Originally conceived during the previous century and designed to operate as either horse or foot soldiers as circumstances required, they were never very successful in the dual role and by the time with which we are concerned they much resembled the horse regiments, being almost as heavily equipped, with ponderous saddlery and uniform, as well as having in addition an infantry musket. With all this paraphernalia they were singularly ill-suited for the performance of any sort of dismounted duty.

We are finally left with the artillery arm, in the forties of the 18th Century substantially the same as it had been at the beginning thereof and as it still was at the end. For a number of years its greatest curse had laid in the proliferation of its types and calibres and one of the most notable improvements current about this time was the beginning of a system of standardisation whereby the number of calibres was drastically reduced, thus providing a highly desirable limit to the numerous varieties of ammunition which had previously to be carried about in the artillery caissons. A stop was thus made to the speedy exhaustion of a particular type of missile and a consequent cessation of function of the relative piece of ordnance at some crucial moment in a battle.

Basically the great majority of cannon in use at this time were smooth bore field guns. They were not especially accurate, throwing a solid ball of iron which was useful against masses of men in that if it hit a formation it could plough through, knocking down men in great numbers. Effective range was not great, being limited primarily by simple deficiency of vision and the consequent inability to 'register' fire. The cannon barrel was smooth and as there was always a tiny interval between the ball and the bore of the piece, some degree of 'windage' resulted causing some inaccuracy in the flight path of the roundshot. For all practical purposes range was therefore shorter than might have been expected, although it increased with the larger guns. This was not actually of much importance, fire being generally opened at little more than six or seven hundred yards. The gunner aimed his cannon for the ball to land just in front of the target formation so that it bounced or 'ricocheted' through the enemy ranks, providing the maximum effect. Lateral error was not too pronounced, and without any device to absorb recoil, each time the gun was fired it bounced back considerably and had to be 'laid' or aimed again. Artillery, nevertheless, was a most important feature of any 18th Century army and became increasingly more so as the years passed.

An alternative to the field gun was provided by the howitzer, although it was used in lesser numbers than the former. The howitzer was, of course, smooth bored and had a short barrel. It threw an explosive shell with a very high trajectory designed to burst on or just above the target. The shell was a hollow iron sphere filled with gunpowder and the howitzer was subject to even greater errors than was the field gun, largely because of the primitive nature of the firing system. A slender tube filled with combustible material and of the appropriate length was inserted into an aperture in the shell before it was loaded into the howitzer barrel. When the piece was fired the flash of the propellant explosion ignited the material in the tube which burned down during the flight and set off the contents of the shell at what was hoped would be the correct moment. In fact the material in the fuse frequently failed to ignite or alternatively burned too quickly, exploding the shell prematurely. The shell might also bury itself in soft ground before the charge exploded, which it would then do with greatly lessened effect. The howitzer was, however, useful in providing a means of indirect fire, for although any system of 'spotting' was pretty rudimentary fire could be brought to bear on enemy troops in a village or behind a wood, and the explosions of the shell in itself was a potent morale factor, particularly in causing panic and disturbance among cavalry and baggage horses.

This has necessarily been a very brief study of the types of troops to be found in a mid-18th Century army and of the weapons used, such as we shall find in 1745 at the Battle of Fontenoy, the engagement chosen for our consideration. In open country, the line of battle of an army consisted of the bulk of infantry in the centre, with cavalry on the wings and possibly in the rear, although the latter was occasionally distributed piece-meal all along the line. Artillery might be deployed on the flanks to provide cross fire against an enemy advance, although from time to time some might also be dis-tributed among the infantry battalions. These served only to increase slightly the infantry fire power and were relatively unimportant, even being at times an impediment to the manoeuvrability of the infantry to whom they were attached. Frequently, of course, more astute generals would take advantage of natural terrain features to heighten their chance of a successful battle, for instance by basing flanks on difficult or impassable obstacles, by fortifying their positions with field entrenchments or by choosing positions on high or rising ground. Fontenoy, as we shall see, was such a battle where a position chosen for its natural strength was increased in defensive power by the construction of man-made features.

Finally, it remains to point out that at the time with which we are concerned, military organisation at the higher level left much to be desired, there being no conception in the field of any military grouping larger than the battalion or squadron. Brigades and divisions, to say nothing of army corps, lay far in the future, and when being given a command, a general was allocated a number of battalions, squadrons and guns, while his staff was very much his own affair, consisting largely of officers of various grades who owed him friendship or allegiance or from whom he expected some sort of preferment. The military system was something of a paradox, although it operated reasonably well in spite of its faults. Lack of a proper system of command did on occasion cause trouble as we shall see in the pages that follow.

4
The Background

The complicated dynastic permutations of the 18th Century monarchical system produced numerous wars, none more characteristic of the epoch in its political manoeuvrings, its frequent diplomatic chicanery and blatant double-dealing, and its formal approach to military operations, than the War of the Austrian Succession, which lasted from 1740 until 1748 and of whose course and main events we must have at least a general knowledge up to the year in which we are particularly interested, that is 1745, when occurred the Battle of Fontenoy. The genesis of the war is to be sought nearly thirty years prior to its actual outbreak, in 1713 to be precise, this being the date of a renowned document the celebrated Pragmatic Sanction.

This prestigious piece of paper took its name from an Act of State of the rulers of the one-time Byzantine Empire and in this instance it was the brain child of Charles VI, the Holy Roman Emperor, whose permanent aim in life – it amounted indeed to a species of obsession – was to ensure that the Imperial succession should fall to his daughter, Maria Theresa, he being without male issue. Although the Emperor was elected by a Diet which met at Frankfurt at the appropriate times and whose members included the rulers of Hanover, Brandenburg and Saxony – who were at the same time, as it happened, the kings of England, Prussia and Poland respectively – the elective process was something of a formality and the office of Emperor had been to all intents and purposes hereditary in the Austrian house of Hapsburg for several hundred years. During this time the family had by various means, largely the common expedient of advantageous political marriages, made itself the rulers of Hungary, Bohemia, parts of northern Italy, and the Low Countries, in addition to its own Austrian lands.

Despite all this apparent power, the Emperor Charles VI seems to have been well aware of the hazardous political climate of the times and almost from the moment he came to the imperial throne he devoted all his energies to making certain that, when the time came, Europe, and in particular the Imperial Diet, would accept his daughter, the lovely and accomplished Maria Theresa, as his successor to that throne. Charles without doubt had few illusions concerning his fellow monarchs and knew well the predatory nature of certain of them and their cheerful disregard of formal and seemingly binding alliances. However, by all sorts of bribery and persuasion he did his best to ensure that all the interested parties subscribed to his Pragmatic Sanction – or in other words guaranteed their support for Maria Theresa when the Emperor died and she had to present herself for election before the Diet at Frankfurt. To the neglect of other and possibly equally important imperial duties Charles finally satisfied himself that there was a general adherence to his document. History, however, was to show that his efforts had been in vain and his hopes illusory, for his death in 1740 was but a signal for the first of what was to be a long succession of storms.

Right speedily claim and counterclaim to the imperial

office were made in all quarters. Bavaria, in the person of her Elector, Charles Albert, with the very powerful support of France, was first in line, but Maria Theresa, now 24 and married to Francis of Lorraine, prepared to defend what she deemed her heritage with admirable courage and vigour. It was not from France nor her Bavarian nominee, however, that the first blow came, but from a completely unexpected quarter – and the unexpected enemy was to prove a deadly and determined one. The enemy in fact was Prussia in the person of King Frederick II, soon to be known as 'the Great', who himself had been but a few months on his own throne.

His background had been a strange one, for his father had despised and quarrelled bitterly with him, had sent him to prison and forced him to watch the execution of a close friend, and in general had treated him abominably and tyrannically. In consequence of all this Frederick had become something of a recluse, reading much and attempting to write poetry, and turning to France and French literature for consolation and inspiration. Voltaire became his friend and encouraged him in his literary aspirations, but no one suspected just what qualities lurked beneath the eccentric surface of the young dilettante, these being revealed only when he had succeeded his father on the latter's death.

Not only did he come to the throne of Prussia but, what was more important, he inherited the finest army in Europe, organised, trained and disciplined by his martinet father, whose passion it had been to watch his giant grenadiers, the famous *Riesengrenadiere*, marching and countermarching on the Potsdam parade grounds. It was not these decorative and militarily useless giants whom the new king seized upon but rather the Prussian army as a whole, and in his able if unscrupulous hands it was for twenty years of warfare to be the wonder of military Europe. Released then from his cruel and possibly near-insane father, Frederick emerged as a consummate soldier and one of the Great Captains of his age – and one with only the slightest pretension to simple morality and honour! Justifying his action by an ancient claim by the Electorate of Brandenburg to certain portions of the Austrian domains in Silesia he invaded that territory with 30,000 men. His irruption into Silesia was well-timed, for most of the European powers who might conceivably have protested were themselves heavily engaged in their own affairs. Russia and Sweden were at war, Poland was in no condition to pose a threat to him, while both Bavaria and Saxony themselves had designs upon Austria. France was bound to support Bavaria, while Great Britain had no continental commitment; indeed the King was also Elector of Hanover and most sensitive to any threat to his European domain.

During the winter of 1740–41 there was little action, the first pitched battle taking place on 10th April, 1741 at Mollwitz, when the Austrians were defeated. To call this a victory for Frederick would be something of a misnomer because his cavalry were driven from the field by the excellent Austrian horse, and the King was carried along in the rout, whether voluntarily or otherwise is a matter of conjecture. The battle, however, was won in his absence by the superb Prussian infantry under Marshal Schwerin. This experience was a terrible and traumatic one for the young King – he was about 30 years of age at the time – but he profited from the lesson immensely in the long years of warfare which lay ahead of him, for what he perhaps imagined was to be a short war with easy pickings, was to endure for nearly a quarter of a century and on more than one occasion to bring Prussia almost to her knees in utter defeat.

In a way, however, the Prussian victory at Mollwitz did benefit Austria, for after some soul-searching Britain resolved to help, and a subsidy of £300,000 was granted to Maria Theresa to assist her in the fight for her inheritance. There was one rather substantial fly in the ointment, however, in the person of King George who, as Elector of Hanover, was throughout this time extremely exercised as to possible harm to his German possessions should they be visited by war. Swallowing his pride with, it seems, little effort, he repudiated the original decision to help Maria Theresa, and when Frederick of Prussia, now allied with France, moved some troops towards Hanover, George II executed a complete volte-face, making haste to wash his hands of Maria's claim and agreeing to support the French interest and candidate, Charles Albert of Bavaria. He also simultaneously assured them of the neutrality of Hanover in the event of further hostilities between Prussia and Austria.

All this was much to the detriment of Maria Theresa's cause and her future at this time seemed to be without promise, particularly as her defeat at Mollwitz had caused the French to speed up warlike preparations obviously intended for a conflict with Austria. By the Treaty of Nymphenberg France formally agreed to support Charles Albert of Bavaria and in June, 1741, when Maria Theresa was crowned Queen of Hungary at Pressburg, a French army was preparing to invade her country under the Duc de Broglie, one of whose cavalry commanders was the Comte de Saxe, of whom we shall hear much more ere long. By the beginning of November this army was at Prague, the capital of Austrian Bohemia, and the city soon fell to the enemy forces, the French and a contingent of Saxons.

Influenced by this, Frederick of Prussia again went into action, marching towards Vienna, but as it happened, the period in which Maria Theresa's fortunes were at their nadir seemed to be ended, for a time at least, and her forces were everywhere on the march, driving the invading French from Austria proper and surging forwards into Bavaria. In fact, when, on 12th February, 1742, Charles Albert of Bavaria was crowned Holy Roman Emperor in Frankfurt, his own capital city of Munich was occupied by a doubtless triumphant army. By July, when this force had swung northwards, the position of the French armies based on Prague had become extremely precarious and they were in ever-growing danger of having their main lines of communication seriously threatened or even completely severed.

Reverses had still to be endured by Maria Theresa, however, and her army was again defeated by Frederick the Great, this time at Chotusitz on 17th May, 1742. Although unequivocally beaten, the Austrians fought with great spirit, both combatant armies suffering 7,000 casualties. At this juncture, such losses were too much for Frederick to bear with equanimity and he decided to bow out of the fighting for the time being. Needless to say, he made sure he was not the loser and by the provisions of the Peace of Breslau, 11th June, 1742, he received most of Silesia, which, after all, had been his primary objective. Saxony also made peace with Austria and the recently crowned Emperor Charles Albert was left with only the active support of France.

By this time, in fact, the entire French army which had been operating in Bohemia had been forced to take refuge in Prague, shut up there by Austrian armies under Prince Francis of Lorraine, husband of Maria Theresa, and General Königsegg. Things rapidly grew desperate within the walls, even the French generals being reduced to subsisting on the most iron of rations. An attempt at a counter-attack by a French army under Marshal Maillebois with the object of relieving the beleaguered garrison proved abortive and the position of the French became even worse. Nevertheless they were able to beat off a determined Austrian assault in August. The crisis was reached on 16th December, when in sub-zero temperatures, 15,000 French troops burst from the city in two huge columns, and brushing aside the Austrian containing force, set off upon a most dreadful retreat, at the end of which the survivors, numbering about a half of the original strength of the army, arrived at Egra. It was an operation not to be equalled until the retreat of the Grand Army from Moscow some seventy years later.

While all this was going on an immense amount of

diplomatic 'coming and going' had been taking place in England. This unprecedented activity was the result of George II having come under the powerful influence of Lord John Carteret, as a result of which the King at last decided on active participation in the European War, by despatching 16,000 British troops to the Low Countries, where they were to be joined by Hessians and Hanoverians. It must be remembered that this country was not officially at war with France and that therefore the planned expeditionary forces to operate against French troops were merely 'auxiliaries' of Maria Theresa, as indeed the French were 'auxiliaries' of Charles Albert. The army was to be largely British, but with Hessian and Hanoverian contingents, and it was to be commanded by the seventy-year-old Earl of Stair, a distinguished soldier who had served with Marlborough, but who had seen no active service since those great days. There was a deal of manoeuvring over the location of the various contingents as they arrived and at the same time plans were considered for action against the enemy.

A number of plans for anti-French operations was put forward, among them being one proposal by the Earl of Stair who proposed that the forces in the Netherlands be ordered to make a direct thrust into France, to Dunkirk and possibly even on to Paris itself! Whatever the merits or demerits of this bold scheme – it seemed that memories of Marlborough's march to the Danube lingered in the old general's mind and he might have contemplated a similar dramatic coup whereby his name would be remembered – the plan, alas, foundered on a number of political rocks, not the least being the King's strong antipathy towards leaving his beloved Electorate of Hanover undefended. The year 1742, therefore, closed without any definite military action being taken.

The campaign of 1743 opened with a vast amount of marching and counter-marching by both the Pragmatic and the French armies, but by the end of June both armies were established on opposite sides of the River Main. The British, Austrians and Hanoverians – now commanded in person by King George, who had arrived accompanied by a prodigious baggage train – lay about Dettingen and Aschaffenburg, while the French, under the command of Marshal de Noailles, were at a distance of only four miles away, on the further side of the river. The Frenchman was a most wily general and while the Pragmatic Army lay before him he prepared a cunning trap. His enemies were, in fact, in a rather precarious position, their supply lines having been cut by the French, and it was decided to retreat to the great magazine at Hanau, where reinforcements were also to be found.

As soon as the movement started Noailles detached a powerful force under the Duc de Grammont to cross the Main at Seligenstadt, some miles in front of the allies, and occupy Dettingen, through which they must pass. At the same time Noailles crossed at Aschaffenburg, coming up in the allied rear, thus effectively trapping King George and his army. Alas for the French marshal's scheme, it was rendered ineffectual by the unwise and precipitate action of de Grammont, who, instead of awaiting the approaching army in a position covered in front by a marsh, with the flanks covered by the River Main on the one side and steep hills on the other, advanced from this superb position to engage the allies on more or less open ground.

What followed was the Battle of Dettingen which was, to use a well-worn phrase, very much a 'soldiers' battle', which means that junior generals, regimental officers and the men themselves, by hard fighting, extricated their superiors from the sticky situation into which the incompetence of the latter had largely pushed them. It ended with King George – both he and his son the Duke of Cumberland had had their horses run away with them during the action – and his army driving the French back through Dettingen and making good their retreat, a most fortunate result, due largely to the imprudence of the Duc de Grammont. There was no pursuit and the battle was followed by more manoeuvring, both military and diplomatic, until the armies went into winter quarters in October, 1743.

5
Before the Battle
❖❖❖❖❖❖❖❖❖

Throughout the year 1744 there was much naval, military and diplomatic activity on all sides, of which possibly the most relevant to our account is a brief consideration of the French attempt to carry out a full-scale invasion of England. Attempt may not indeed be the correct term, for in modern parlance the enterprise 'hardly got off the ground'! In short, the plan was instigated by Cardinal Tencin, Louis XV's principal adviser, who was of the opinion that a substantial French army landing in England would be sufficient to cause a general revolution in favour of the exiled Stuart king, whose cause he particularly favoured. To this end it was arranged that upwards of 15,000 troops should concentrate in northern France, while transports and other sorts of shipping were assembled at Dunkirk to ferry them across the Channel.

Naval squadrons were alerted to afford protection to the transports as they made the crossing, and Marshal Saxe was given command of the expedition. Prince Charles Edward, elder son of the 'Old Pretender', made his way to Dunkirk, and all seemed ready for the plan to be put into operation. Some 7,000 men were initially embarked, but the covering French fleet was frightened back to its base by the appearance of some British ships of the line, and almost at the same moment the Channel gales once again came to the assistance of the island race, the French transports – together with their unfortunate occupants – being sorely battered by a tremendous storm. Many ships were sunk and numbers of troops lost. The vessels which escaped made a painful way back to Dunkirk with the greatest alacrity of which they were capable. Charles Edward made his disgruntled way back to Paris and the invasion plan as it existed was abandoned.

Before this, as it happened, France had earlier formally declared war on Great Britain – on 15th March, 1744, to be exact – but no military operations of real importance to us took place during the summer, and the armies, as was customary, went into winter quarters in October. Marshal Wade, who had commanded the allied army in the Low Countries, returned home, having resigned the command, while his opposite number, Marshal Saxe, repaired to Paris, there to prepare a plan for the campaign of 1745.

During the ensuing winter many of the great European capitals were the scene of even more diplomatic activity which culminated in the signing, on 8th January, 1745, of a four party alliance between Great Britain, Austria, Holland and Saxony. This took place at Warsaw. Among the provisions of the treaty was one whereby the already existing subsidy to Maria Theresa was increased to half a million pounds, and some considerable consideration was devoted to the disposition and composition of the army which was to take the field against France during the coming campaign. What appeared most important, following the principles of the age, was the decision as to the identity of the general who was to be appointed Commander-in-Chief of the allied forces. After lengthy discussion, to this post was appointed His Royal Highness the Duke of Cumberland, son of King George. In actual rank a major-general, and a fairly junior one to boot, he arrived at the Hague to take up his appointment on 17th April, 1745. From the Hague he proceeded to join his army. Cumberland was a young man of 28 at this time and the two other generals who formed with him a species of triumvirate were the Austrian Count Königsegg, a septuagenarian of very uncertain health, and the Prince of Waldeck, about the same age as the Duke, who commanded the numerous Dutch troops forming part of the Pragmatic Army.

Nor had the French High Command been dormant during the winter months, and with Saxe's inspiration a great deal was done to bring the army up to strength and to train it for the fighting which lay ahead. The Marshal's own health deteriorated very considerably during this time and he had the services of a veritable corps of doctors who laboured to restore his once powerful body to some semblance of its former strength – a somewhat formidable task, in view of the frenetic sort of life the patient had enjoyed for a number of years.

One fairly important event did occur right at the beginning of the year 1745, Charles Albert, Elector of Bavaria and elected Holy Roman Emperor dying at the end of January. In consequence of his demise it seemed that Maria Theresa's husband, Francis of Lorraine, would be the logical choice for the Imperial throne. As if in celebration of this, the increasingly successful Austrian armies had, by March, overrun that part of Bavaria not in their possession and had driven the new Elector of Bavaria – successor to the late Charles Albert – from his capital at Munich. This was too much for the new ruler and within a month he had concluded a peace with Maria Theresa – on 15th April – thus releasing a large proportion of the Austrian army for action against France.

In these circumstances, looking at his one-time allies, Louis XV of France found himself in a somewhat isolated position, particularly since, with some perception, he realised he could not wholly rely on Frederick the Great, whose policy was increasingly one of complete self-interest. In consequence of this, Louis made certain peace proposals. These were forthwith rejected by the interested countries as being completely unacceptable and the French King had no option but to gird his loins for battle, stirring his ordinarily lethargic nature into commendable activity and making a powerful effort to ensure a successful campaign in the coming fighting season. To this end he maintained in the principal command of his army the redoubtable Maurice de Saxe, whom we have already met more than once in these pages and who merits a few words of description at this stage.

He was the illegitimate son of an Elector of Saxony and the famous beauty, Aurora von Königsmarck, and he provides a most striking picture of the archetypal soldier of fortune. His life was full in every sense of the phrase and as a result of what might be politely termed his earlier excesses – wine and women in particular – his health was far from good, despite his being only some fifty years of age. Severe dropsy was a constant source of pain and a most severe handicap to him. Indeed, at this time he was suffering from a particularly severe bout of the complaint, and it was rumoured in the allied camp that his death was momentarily expected. These sanguine hopes proved to be without foundation – unfortunately for the allied cause – and by 20th April he was at his field headquarters at Maubege, where he was able at first hand to examine his troops and assess his army's capabilities. His force was a most substantial one, its numbers amounting to about 70,000 infantry and over 25,000 cavalry.

Saxe's initial objective – following the customary strategy of the time – was to seize an important fortress, and his target was therefore Tournai, one of the most technically advanced defensive installations, conceived and developed by the famous Vauban, most celebrated military engineer of the century. To conceal his plan and preliminary movements from the Allies, however, he

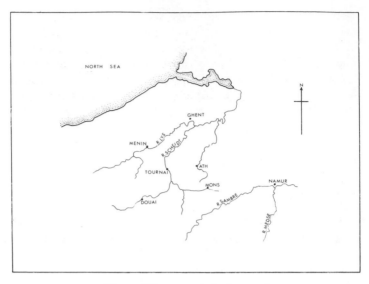

Map 1. The strategic background

sent a strong diversionary force towards another strong town – this being Mons – while he moved in person with his main body towards Tournai, held in some strength by a garrison of Dutch troops, numbering in the neighbourhood of 7,000 men.

Although a fairly elementary piece of strategy, Saxe's feint was completely successful. The Allied generals were taken in by the diversionary movement and, encompassed as they were in a thick fog of war, it was a profound shock to them when, on 28th April, they were informed that the entire French army lay before Tournai, which they well knew to be probably the most important fortress in the area, controlling the most advantageous route into Flanders. In all fairness, however, it must be said that recovery was prompt, and on the following day orders were issued for the march of the Allied army. An accession of Hessian infantry and cavalry had raised the total strength of the troops under Cumberland's command to about 53,000 men – British, Dutch, German and Austrian. As we have seen, at this time Saxe deployed something like 70,000. The disparity in the numbers need not be over-emphasised, however, as a considerable proportion of the French troops were not available for field operations, being ensconced around Tournai as the blockading force. The leading elements of Cumberland's army, marching with some deliberation and further delayed by bad weather, arrived at Maubege on 6th May.

Meantime, Saxe had been far from idle, sending reconnaissance forces far and wide to probe the enemy's intentions and, already armed with the most accurate information concerning the strength and progress of the Allied army, had decided upon where his battle would be fought. Happy is the general, obviously, who can, at his leisure, choose the very stretch of terrain where he considers that his army will have the best chance of success, and then can force his enemy into fighting on that very ground. Initially at least it was to be a purely defensive action and to this end Saxe decided upon a most powerful position; indeed so strong was it that a less imprudent and headstrong general than Cumberland might well have been considerably reluctant to essay any sort of frontal attack upon it.

The position – and what was in effect to be the battle-field of Fontenoy – lay a few miles south-east of the Tournai fortress and was based firmly upon the River Scheldt. The line of battle as drawn out by Saxe was a species of capital 'L', the contained angle being fractionally greater than a right angle. The upper extremity of the vertical of the 'L' rested on the village of Anthoing on the river itself, the apex of the angle on the village of Fontenoy, while the other extremity of the horizontal touched one end of the great Wood of Barry. No attempt was made by Saxe to link these three points with any sort of continuous line of entrenchments of field fortifications, as it seems that he was strongly of the opinion that a single line, once breached, is useless, since the troops who have passed through the gap are immediately able to take the defenders in flank and rear. Thus, what he opted for was a series of individual and self-contained small redoubts. Each could be defended independently and all could be mutually supporting. Any enemy passing between them would be subjected to very effective cross fire from the garrisons of the redoubts.

So, following the Marshal's instructions, the village of Fontenoy itself was fortified and the walls of the houses loop-holed for musketry, forming in itself a redoubt capable of accommodating a considerable body of infantry and its supporting artillery. Considerable attention was paid to the village, for it was without a doubt the key to the entire defensive system. It has been said that some trenches were dug between Fontenoy and the Wood of Barry, but if this is correct their effect on the action to follow was negligible and indeed they probably did not exist, some witnesses and later historians possibly confusing a hollow road running northeast from the village with prepared trenches. In fact, to an enemy approaching up the slope to the Fontenoy–Wood of Barry line nothing was to be seen of any defences, but what was unobservable was of fundamental importance.

Behind the wood Saxe had caused to be erected two redoubts in a position to allow their guns to sweep the approach ground to the position, giving it the effect of a natural glacis or field of fire, which was covered by the Fontenoy guns as well as those from the redoubts. The nearer of the two redoubts became known as the Redoubt d'Eu and its presence was not revealed to the allied army by its initial examination of the ground. The other arm of the 'L' – that from Fontenoy to Anthoing on the Scheldt was also carefully prepared by Saxe, three more or less equidistant redoubts being erected there. They were important in the event of any attack from this quarter, although the likelihood of such an assault was less, as this quarter of the field could also be swept by artillery firing from across the Scheldt.

All in all, the position chosen by Saxe was a very strong one, so much so indeed that it might have caused many an army to sheer off and avoid combat. In the absence of written plans by the commanders involved, it is a facile proceeding, when armed with hindsight, to impute to such generals a far greater strategical and tactical ability than they might actually have possessed. Hence, it is easy to jump to the conclusion that Saxe refrained from taking what might have seemed the obvious course of covering the ground between Fontenoy and the Wood of Barry by the erection of one or more redoubts, feeling that, as traditionally the right wing of an army – in this case the British – was the most powerful, it would be from this direction that the main attack would come and that it would be guided by the terrain into the intense cross-fire from Fontenoy and the Redoubt d'Eu, before it came face to face with a powerful infantry stationed slightly to the rear of these strong points. In other words it would be lured into the unenviable position of being caught in a re-entrant angle. Be that as it may, and whether or not we impute to Saxe an unlikely degree of military insight, there could have been no doubt whence would come the attack, particularly in view of the strong cover to the French right flank provided by the guns across the Scheldt.

In any event, the Allied Army finally came within musket range of the French advanced guards during the evening of 9th May, taking up a position between the villages of Maubrai and Baugnies. Cumberland's command post was established at Broeffel, some little distance to the rear. Once the camp had been established, the three Allied generals mounted their horses and rode off to make as detailed a reconnaissance as possible of the ground occupied by the enemy. No attempt was made to conceal the high rank of the members of the scouting party, a thing more than difficult in itself as the escort to the illustrious trio consisted of no less than twelve squadrons of cavalry. Obviously such a considerable force could not hope to approach really close to the enemy's lines so the view must have been very limited. Although it was discovered that the village of Vezon, which lay in wooded and rough country, was held by the enemy, little could be discerned of what lay beyond.

The following day the generals conferred together at their headquarters, coming to the conclusion that Vezon had to be cleared of the enemy forthwith. Thus, about 10 o'clock, a force of six battalions of infantry and twelve squadrons of cavalry, plus pioneers and some artillery, was assembled and directed forward under the combined command of Lord Crawford and the Hanoverian Brigadier General Roseberg. The troops advanced boldly and after some desultory fire the French occupying Vezon evacuated the village, which was promptly occupied by the Allied infantry. Cumberland thereupon moved his headquarters thither from Bruffoel. At this stage he was strongly advised to push strong parties into the depths of the Wood of Barry lying to his right front, this being obviously occupied by the enemy, but this he failed to do, with unfortunate results.

By this time the day was well advanced, and there remained insufficient time for major operations to be carried out, but an attack would be launched the following day, 11th May. While a diversionary attack would be made on the extreme left flank, at Anthoing, the Dutch in strength would make an assault on Fontenoy village itself, while the main blow would be struck by the British and Hanoverians against the French line between Fontenoy and the Wood of Barry, thus fulfilling what might well have been Saxe's expectations. The march was to begin at 2 a.m. the following morning.

6
Dispositions

◇◆◇◆◇◆◇◆◇

Before proceeding further it might be as well to examine in some detail the composition of the armies
who fought the Battle of Fontenoy and at the same time
to indicate their general dispositions at the outset of the
engagement. Taking the Allied army first, then, we find
that in round numbers the total fighting men deployed
by Cumberland and his associated generals was some
47,000. The army was divided into two wings, one
commanded immediately by Cumberland and
Königsegg and consisting of British and Hanoverian
troops, along with a few Austrians, made up of 25
battalions of foot and 45 squadrons of cavalry, these
numbering 16,500 and 6,750 respectively. The other
wing – the Dutch under the Prince of Waldeck – consisted of 27 infantry battalions (17,550 men) and 40
squadrons of horse (6,000). Thus the two wings were of
nearly equal strength although, as time will reveal, one
performed much more stoutly than the other. In point
of fact it was the British and Hanoverians who formed
the bulk of the right wing, the Austrian contingent being

a relatively small one. The Allied artillery, a very important arm, numbered 80 guns ranging in calibre from the $1\frac{1}{2}$ to the 6 pounder.

Deploying this very considerable army – large even by contemporary standards – was a time-consuming operation and it was this lengthy process which had so delayed operations during the previous day. The 'drawing out' of the army, however, had been completed satisfactorily, well concealed from enemy observation by the woods around Vezon, now in Allied possession. Details of the deployment, beginning with the right wing, which concerns us more closely, was thus: on the extreme right, and, possibly as an afterthought on the part of Cumber-

Fig. 4. Private, The Black Watch (British)

56

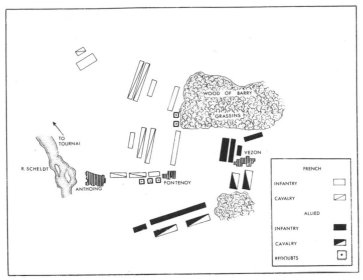

Map 2. Fontenoy – the initial position

land, facing the Wood of Barry was the redoubtable
Black Watch, the Royal Highlanders, with a couple of
so-called 'Free Companies', continental troops of
uncertain quality and indeterminate origin. Two hundred yards to their left stood the main line of battle,
formed by two massive rows of infantry. The first of
these consisted of the Guards Brigade – taking pride of
place in the extreme right of the front line – with two
further infantry brigades, those of Generals Ponsonby
and Onslow, on their left. The second line was formed
of three further brigades, commanded by Generals
Howard, Bland and Skelton. The Hanoverian infantry,
under General Zastrow, was positioned on the British
left, with its own cavalry supporting it to the rear. Still
further to the left stood the Dutch infantry, with their
cavalry forming up on the extreme left of the entire
Allied line. It was in these positions that the men lay
upon their arms for their short period of repose prior to
standing to in the early hours of the morning for the
crucial hours lying ahead.

Meantime Marshal Saxe had more or less completed the dispositions of his army to his personal satisfaction, and his units – almost entirely the cream of the oldest French regiments, many with a century or more of fighting history behind them – had taken up their designated positions. The Marshal was naturally handicapped by having to leave a very substantial containing force to prevent any possible sallies by the garrison of Tournai, in all something like 21,000 men. This left in very round numbers something like 60,000 soldiers to man the Anthoing–Fontenoy–Wood of Barry position, along which, broadly speaking, the troops were thus arrayed. First of all, of course, like the prudent general he was, Saxe left nothing to chance, even the possibility of a hasty retreat and he had had three fortified bridges erected across the Scheldt directly in his rear, these being guarded by three battalions of infantry, drawn from the French and Swiss Guards. Starting from the Anthoing extremity of the French line, then, that village itself was garrisoned by five battalions (four from the veteran Piedmont regiment and one of Royal La Marine), four further battalions from the Crillon and Biron regiments linking Anthoing with Fontenoy, which itself was packed with soldiery, two battalions from the Regiment Le Roi and one of the Swiss regiment of Diesbach. In accordance with his plan, the Marshal deployed in what was to be a species of 'killing ground', that area between Fontenoy and the Wood of Barry some of the best battalions he had in hand, thirteen in number. They included four of the celebrated Gardes Françaises and two of the Gardes Suisses, the others being drawn from Aubeterre and Courten. Some six hundred yards to the rear of this infantry line stood the bulk of the French cavalry and again behind them stood the glittering squadrons of the famous Maison du Roi – the Household Cavalry of the Kings of France, Gendarmerie du Roi, Mousquetaires, Gardes du Corps and others equally as renowned. Three regiments of dragoons – Bauffremont, Royal and Mestre de Camp – were deployed to support the infantry between Anthoing and Fontenoy. The redoubts guarding the fringe of the Wood of Barry furthest from the Allied army were well garrisoned, the nearer being held by the Regiment d'Eu, hence of course the name whereby it has become famous in military history.

Closer to the Allied troops the Wood of Barry itself was thick with French light troops, especially the fringes, where the renowned Arquebussiers de Grassin kept vigil.

To the left rear of the French position lay the village of Ramecroix, which was covered by wooded and marshy terrain and close to which stood the left flanking French unit, the Royal Corse infantry, in front of which stood the main body of Saxe's reserve infantry, consisting mainly of the six battalions of the Irish Brigade in the

Fig. 5. Private soldier, Gardes Françaises (French)

French service, the legendary 'Wild Geese'. Some light field works had been erected at this point and the Irishmen were supported by eight pieces of artillery. Another very senior infantry regiment, Normandie, was also close at hand. Still further to the rear and watching the bridges over the Scheldt were seven more battalions from the Touraine and Auvergne regiments, together with several squadrons of cuirassiers.

It should be noted that the reserve infantry were well placed either to support the French centre should it come under undue pressure or to deal with any enemy troops who might push through and emerge from the Wood of Barry.

It was therefore in this splendid and well defended position that Marshal Saxe and his army awaited the attack. It was really a superb example of defence according to the thinking of the time, and without doubt it stemmed from the Marshal's own experience many years before at the Battle of Malplaquet, where he had seen some of his earliest military service. There a continuous line of breastworks stretching between two woods and deemed to be invulnerable to infantry attack had been broken and had thereafter been useless to the defence as the assaulting troops had poured through the gap. As we have already mentioned there is the possibility that Saxe made no attempt to raise any earthworks on the Fontenoy–Wood of Barry line on the assumption that when the attack was delivered in this quarter – he was certain that it would be – the cross-fire from his skilfully-placed redoubts and the village of Fontenoy would scourge the enemy beyond endurance and make them easy prey for the counterattack which would come from the strong infantry line he had placed a little to the rear of the line. That the attack, when it did come, was delivered with such determination and penetrated so far into the French position is no reflection on his judgement and sense of tactics but is rather a most striking commentary on the discipline and fortitude of the infantry making it, no less than on the appalling lack

60

of tactical knowledge on the part of the general who ordered it.

On this note, indeed, with the armies poised for action and undoubtedly the greatest tension and excitement everywhere, it might be appropriate to make a few final brief comments on the generals involved in the battle, notably the two commanders-in-chief. As it happened, Louis XV of France was in person with his army – his numerous courtiers and other hangers-on being the greatest possible nuisance to Saxe – but he wisely left its direction to his Marshal, and although the Allied command seems to have been officially a species of triumvirate, there is no doubt that the loudest and most potent voice in its councils was that of the Duke of Cumberland. This individual was without doubt one of the most consistently unsuccessful generals ever to have commanded a British army in the field, his sole recorded success being the Battle of Culloden in the year after Fontenoy, when, with an excellent army of highly trained professional soldiers – horse, foot and guns – he defeated little more than half their number of ill-armed, poorly disciplined and exhausted Highlanders, who sacrificed themselves in the last effort of the exiled Stuart monarch to regain his throne.

It would appear that, in general, Cumberland subscribed to the belief that his royal birth automatically conferred upon him a high degree of strategic and tactical skill, which delusion, despite his experience at Fontenoy – unfortunate, as we shall see – was never quite dispelled. Apart from this, his name must forever be associated with the atrocities perpetrated in the name of the British Government against the defeated Jacobites, and his soubriquet of 'The Butcher' was doubtless well deserved, although, truth to tell, he was but one of a number whose excesses became notorious. In any event, he was again in command of an allied army at Hastenbeck in 1757 and was yet once more soundly beaten, after which he signed the less than honourable Convention of Kloster Seven. Following this he was subjected to so much pressure and general obloquy that he resigned all his appointments and died in comparative obscurity in 1765 at the age of 44.

We need say little concerning Cumberland's brother generals, the youthful Dutchman, the Prince of Waldeck, an impetuous young man of no great military ability who appears to have been well and truly dominated by Cumberland, and Count Königsegg, the Austrian Field Marshal who had served notably well in some of the previous wars of the Empire but was now nearly 73 and an invalid to boot. He was not best qualified to counteract the enthusiasm of his younger colleagues. Having disposed of these a trifle summarily, it must be fair if we notice one or two of the subordinate generals, in whom lay the greater strength of the command structure. First, and by far the most capable as well as the most distinguished, was Sir John Ligonier, an exiled Frenchman, a Huguenot, who had adopted Britain as his native country and who served her with the greatest loyalty for many years. Commissioned into the British Army as early as 1703 he was present at all the great battles fought by the Duke of Marlborough, and became a splendid leader of cavalry, his own regiment, the 8th Horse – which became known as the Black Guards by reason of its high reputation as well as the black colour of its regimental facings – being famous throughout the army. His influence upon the British Army was very considerable and there seems little doubt that he was the ablest British general of his time. Despite his cavalry background, he was General of Foot at Fontenoy, while Sir James Campbell, himself a competent leader of mounted troops, was General of Horse. There remains but one other of whom we should take some cognizance, as we shall encounter him later. This is Brigadier General James Ingoldsby, 'an amiable man of convivial habits' as he was later described. He seems to have been something of a drinking companion of the Duke of Cumberland, whose preference for him was, as it proved, as much a cause of the unfortunate result of the battle as was his own military deficiency. Ingoldsby combined want of decision with a complete inability to assess a military situation, plus a reluctance to obey orders unless they came from the very mouth of the Commander-in-Chief – and even then not too readily!

We have already spoken of Saxe. As we have noted, he was the illegitimate son of the Elector Augustus of Saxony, and had started his military career in the Imperial Army, but, making his way to France in 1721 he had purchased there the colonelcy of a foreign regiment in that country's service. In 1726 he stood as one of the candidates for the vacant Duchy of Courland, being equally successful in the election. Caught, however, between pressure exerted from both Poland and Russia he was obliged to give up his newly-won duchy and return to Paris. Following this he became notorious for the disorderly nature of his way of life and it seems that he was at least as famous as a lover as he was as a soldier. After a severe illness in 1732 he fought in the armies of the Duke of Berwick and of the Marshal de Noailles, reaching the rank of lieutenant general by 1736. Serving in the numerous campaigns which he had, and living at the hectic pace which was his custom, his health – although he was a powerfully built man – began to deteriorate and, *inter alia* he was the victim of a painful form of dropsy by the time of his early middle-age. Nevertheless his mind was of the keenest, and during the illness already referred to, he wrote a strikingly original work of military theory – published after his death under the title of *Mes Reveries*.

Of Saxe's subordinates, we need note only another foreigner in French service, the Marshal Count von Löwendahl. Like Saxe, the bend sinister figured in his ancestry, his father being a natural son of the Danish King, Frederick I. Like Saxe, too, he had fought in every war he could find, seeing early service with the Danish and Russian armies before joining that of the King of France. He was a specialist in siegecraft and a devoted subordinate of the Marshal.

7
The Battle

Little rest could have been the lot of the Allied troops during the night for by 2 a.m. the following morning – 11th May – the entire army was on the move. Getting about in what must be considered to be total darkness is a fatiguing and unnerving operation – units go astray, guides fail to appear at the appointed time and place, troops collide with each other in spite of the most careful planning, there are alarms and excursions, and nerves become taut and frayed. There are lengthy periods of waiting and everything combines to dampen the spirits and wear down men heavily burdened with arms and equipment, who well know that doubtless daylight will bring violent action and possible sudden death, and who are keenly aware that their generals are committed to a frontal attack on a strong position.

In this particular case movement was further hampered by the troops' having to pass through the wooded and very difficult stretch of ground lying around and beyond Vezon. Some reconnaissances had been pushed forward, however, and at about 4 a.m. the Duke of

Cumberland's advance was brought to a sudden halt by the intelligence that at least one strong and well-garrisoned redoubt was located on the further edge of the Wood of Barry, where its formidable presence was going to be an obvious hindrance to any advance in this quarter. It was at once apparent that some considerable re-thinking would have to be done. Cumberland's decision to conduct an offensive battle was not altered, however, and immediate arrangements were put into force to neutralise this dangerous field fortification. It seemed, too, that not a little opposition was to be experienced from the wood itself where light infantrymen were much

Fig. 6. Trooper, Royal North British Dragoons (British)

in evidence, these of course being the Arquebussiers de Grassin.

To deal with this unexpected contretemps then, a task force was organised on the extreme right wing of the Allied army. It consisted of four battalions of infantry – the 12th Foot (Duroure's); the 13th Foot (Pulteney's); the Black Watch, and the Hanoverian regiment of Böschlanger. In command of this group was placed the officer to whom reference has already been made: Brigadier General Ingoldsby. He was ordered to clear the wood and deal with the redoubt or redoubts at its further extremity, his action being timed to coincide with a strong Dutch attack on the other wing, against the villages of Anthoing and Fontenoy. These movements were to be followed up by a direct assault on the centre of the enemy left by British and Hanoverian infantry advancing up the gentle slope towards the apparently lightly-held ground between Fontenoy and the Wood of Barry. However, in plain terms Ingoldsby was not the man for the job and he failed miserably to carry out his orders and may not even have understood the importance of the mission entrusted to him.

In any case, while he was going through the motions of getting his extempore brigade under way dawn broke and with this first light the French batteries in Fontenoy and the redoubts opened fire with round shot. Fifteen squadrons of British cavalry had previously been brought forward into open ground to screen the British and Hanoverian infantry emerging from the Vezon woods and enclosures to deploy into formation for attack, and despite the still poor visibility and the wisps of early morning mist lingering in the hollows and around the trees the French cannon balls began quickly to bound and ricochet through the lines of cavalry, causing severe losses. Of these none was more of a blow to Cumberland than the mortal wounding of Sir James Campbell, his General of Horse. His fall caused much confusion and it was some time before the chain of command could be re-established, during which period the cavalry had to stand fast under this heavy fire, a most harrowing and deadly experience. Cumberland did arrange to have some artillery moved forward to reply to the French fire but again this took time. The mass of soldiery assembling for the assault was very considerable and the guns experienced difficulty in finding gaps and getting through to their designated stations. In effect it was a full hour before they were able to take up their battery position and open fire. One minor success was achieved almost immediately, as it happened, this being the killing of the Duc de Grammont, the French general whose rash advance to meet the army of King George in open ground, instead of awaiting the latter's arrival in a near impregnable position, had resulted in the French defeat at Dettingen two years previously.

As the opposing guns continued their thunderous duel, and as the British and Hanoverian battalions marched and counter-marched in the complicated process of deploying into battle order, we must again turn our attention to the Allied right wing, where we left Brigadier General Ingoldsby arranging his four battalion task force for its advance to clear the Wood of Barry and thereafter to engage the attention of the two redoubts at its further extremity. The fire from the main redoubt continued to plough through the Allied ranks and from the edges of the wood itself came unceasing musketry from the Arquebussiers de Grassin positioned there All things considered, their presence had an effect quite out of proportion to the size of the unit.

Earlier, about 6 a.m., Ingoldsby had, in fact, moved forward with his brigade but at once came under fire from the Redoubt d'Eu and from the aforementioned Grassins. His orders were, it appears, to advance up to the French battery – that is, the Redoubt – occupy it and seize the cannon it contained. It was deemed possible that the cannon might be turned on the enemy were this achieved and some men from the train of artillery were detailed to accompany the column with this in mind. Alas, however, as soon as the enemy fire was felt,

Ingoldsby halted the column in a hollow road leading towards the Wood of Barry and there he seems to have remained in utter indecision. He was a soldier of some service and it seems inconceivable that there was any pusillanimous or dishonourable reason for his extraordinary behaviour, any more than there was for the refusal of Lord George Sackville to bring his cavalry into action against the French at the Battle of Minden in 1759 – it seems that some sort of paralysis of mind seized both these generals. Ingoldsby did, however, send forward a reconnaissance towards the wood, and not liking what he learned when it returned, despatched a staff officer to the Duke of Cumberland to ask for artillery support, and while awaiting a reply to his request, indulged in the traditional recourse of the indecisive general by holding a sort of council of war, whereat he asked the opinions of his senior officers.

Sir Robert Munro of Foulis, commanding the Black Watch, suggested that his own regiment, being well capable of this sort of independent action, should advance forthwith into the wood and clear the Grassins from it, preparatory to an advance by the entire force through the said wood and on to the redoubt which was the ultimate objective. This proposal seems to have met with some sort of approval from Ingoldsby, but he took no immediate action to put it into effect and meantime the artillery he had asked for arrived in the shape of three 6-pounders. These guns came quickly into action, firing canister into the wood, not the ideal sort of ammunition for this sort of work but it was probably sufficient to drive the Grassins further back into the depths. This took place under the eye of Cumberland himself, he having followed the guns to see what was actually afoot. At this point, possibly activated by the presence of the Commander-in-Chief, Ingoldsby re-formed his brigade, with Duroure's Regiment and the Black Watch in the front line, with the other two infantry battalions forming a second rank, and again a deliberate advance began. At this point Cumberland unluckily moved away from the immediate operational area and almost at once Ingoldsby again halted his men, having noted that a considerable number of Grassins was again in evidence in the wood.

This renewed lack of activity on the part of his right flank task force again became apparent to Cumberland and about 8 o'clock, when the artillery had been firing for about two hours, he realised that something was seriously amiss. Once more he repaired to his extreme right wing where he found Ingoldsby's brigade virtually in the same position where he had seen it last. It would seem strange if the royal temper did not explode with some violence at this point, but no details are available of the resulting conversation between him and the reluctant Ingoldsby, none of his staff having remained, probably wisely, within earshot. Whatever transpired, Cumberland again left Ingoldsby and went off to take up a more central position on the battlefield. Whether the fiasco was entirely due to the reluctance of Ingoldsby personally to act, or whether it was due to his lack of appreciation of how vitally important was the successful execution of the mission entrusted to him, or whether he privately deemed too difficult the forcing of a passage through the wood and a subsequent assault upon a fortification will never be known, but whatever the truth of the matter, there he and his force remained for the time being.

There was no want of action on the far left of the Allied line, however, the Prince of Waldeck urging forward towards Fontenoy his columns of Dutch infantry with cavalry in immediate support. Apparently the young Prince was unaware of the strength of the French defences – he had apparently done no personal reconnaissance of his objective – and his troops, scourged by canister and musketry from both Fontenoy and Anthoing, at the same time received a heavy enfilading fire from the big guns firing from beyond the River Scheldt. Substantial casualties were inflicted upon them and the entire attacking force recoiled in the greatest confusion, some few actually fleeing completely away from the scene of battle. The bulk of the regiments did halt and turn to face the enemy. There they stood, their presence having little influence on the subsequent course of the battle. After this reverse it appears that Cumberland again contemplated a fresh effort to get his right wing to attack, sending further orders to Ingoldsby, but other events nullified this attempt and nothing transpired.

Time was passing and it was now about 9 a.m. Cumberland's position and indeed that of the Allied army was an unenviable one. The plan to neutralise the threat to the right flank of the Allied army from the Wood of Barry and the redoubt had proved abortive and the strong attempt on the left wing by the Dutch had been stopped dead in its tracks. There was no doubt that it was the time for a decision – one way or the other – to be made, and Cumberland, in association with is fellow general Königsegg, made one, although there would appear to be little doubt that the former, with his youth and determination, was largely responsible for it.

Whatever the pros and cons of how the decision was reached, the die was cast, and arrangements were at once made for one grand and massive attack to be put into operation. It was to be carried out in conjunction with a new movement by the Dutch against Fontenoy, and to this end it was deemed necessary for them to be stiffened by British infantry reinforcements. In consequence the Black Watch and possibly Duroure's Regiment were ordered to be detached from Ingoldsby's brigade and to be moved to the left to join the Dutch infantry. Moving quickly from one wing to the other and, it seems, without waiting for the Dutch, the Black Watch mounted an immediate assault on the village, Sir Robert Munro's request that his regiment be allowed to use their claymores having been granted.

The Highlanders rushed forward, losing heavily from fire from the village, and actually reached the entrenchments, but faced with a deadly hail of musket balls from the massed French infantry within, they were forced to retreat, their Colonel, Sir Robert Munro, being so bulky a man that he had to be carried to the rear by a party of his men. After this repulse the Highlanders waited in vain for the Dutch to put in their own attack, but the latter were far from eager and indeed fell further back themselves at the Highlanders' reverse, the attack from this quarter seeming finally to have been abandoned. So also was the ill-fated right flank movement, which finally came to an ignominious end when Ingoldsby himself was slightly wounded and carried to the rear. Succeeding him as next senior officer was the Hanoverian general Zastrow, who ordered the two remaining regiments of the brigade to form on Skelton's brigade to their left.

While this was taking place, the main attack had itself finally been launched, more than 15,000 infantry marching forward. It is not by any means easy to be definite about the formation adopted by this mass of men – as customary in such cases, many accounts being at variance – but it seems probable that initially the force consisted of two ranks of battalions – seventeen actually being British – but as they advanced and the terrain narrowed, the units became exceedingly compressed, certain of the battalions being obliged to drop back to form a third line. It seems to have been in such a three rank formation that this grand attack was finally delivered. With them the infantrymen manhandled a dozen 6-pounder field guns, a laborious proceeding and much more of an encumbrance in the circumstances than a benefit.

And so, steadily up the long, gentle slope towards the level ground between Fontenoy and the Redoubt d'Eu moved the dense mass of men, forming as they did so, as ideal a target for artillery firing at close range as could be conceived. The fire was murderous, canister and roundshot cutting down the closely arrayed infantrymen in dozens. As they moved further up the slope the target they offered grew denser and even better from the French point of view as the front compressed with the narrowing of the funnel into which they were advancing. Finally, it seems that only six battalions were able to march abreast, their ranks dressing and closing steadily despite the ghastly losses they were incurring. After an appalling progress of nearly half a mile they came up to the ground between Fontenoy and the Redoubt d'Eu where they were exposed to a perfect cross fire, but nevertheless the battalions pressed on, never firing a shot until at last – it would be about 11 a.m. – they came face to face with the long lines of red, blue and white clad enemy – Gardes Suisses, Gardes Françaises and the Aubeterre and Courten infantry regiments. At this most crucial moment of the battle a scant thirty or forty yards separated the two lines of men.

It was here that occurred the famous incident which has doubtless grown greatly in the telling, and whose fame is due largely to that magnificent story teller, Voltaire, who said that an English officer, Lord Charles Hay, stepped forward from the ranks of the First Guards, and having saluted and drunk a toast to the dumbfounded French, asked them to fire first! A dramatic but largely apocryphal tale, although certainly having some slight basis in fact, possibly a young officer's quaffing a libation prior to getting down to the serious business – a touch of bravado, no doubt. Whatever the truth of the incident, certain it is that from the French came a volley, but it was a ragged and uncertain one. There seems scant doubt but that they were taken aback by the frightening, inexorable advance of such a great scarlet-clad body of men, and their fire was largely ineffectual. However, from the British lines there immediately rang out a prodigious and incredibly devastating volley – or series of volleys in the quickest succession – such as had rarely been witnessed upon a battlefield and indeed was not to be repeated until with a single similar volley Wolfe's men destroyed Montcalm's army upon the Heights of Abraham fourteen years later.

It was a tremendous and concentrated hurricane of lead which shattered the French front line, hundreds of men falling before it – in his *History of the British Army* Fortescue claims that the figure was 700 for the Gardes Françaises alone, but gives no authority for this claim. It was the British 1st, 2nd and 3rd Guards whose musketry caused the initial havoc, the French array quite disintegrating as the component regiments melted away in ruin. Even supporting infantry like the Regiments du Roi and Royal, which had been brought up by Marshal Saxe while the Allied infantry was still advancing, were driven to the rear. Forward, following this spectacular blow, went Cumberland's battalions, and after a momentary pause caused by redoubled fire from the Redoubt d'Eu, the great column moved still

Fig. 7. Officer,
Gardes du Corps,
Maison du Roi
(French)

further into the French position until it seemed to grind to a halt some 300 yards beyond the spot where the French front line had stood. Doubtless it seemed to Cumberland, and no doubt to the army as a whole, that the day had been won. This, unfortunately, was only a passing flush of victory and the grim reality came crowding fast upon the Commander-in-Chief, as it became rapidly apparent that the position of his infantry was one of total isolation and imminent danger.

Saxe's plan – if, indeed, it had been to lure the Allies into an impossible situation – had been almost too successful, and he had not counted upon the battle discipline and unprecedented staunchness of his enemy. Nevertheless it was now evident that he could, despite the fracture of his line of infantry, send against them counter-attacks from three directions. This he at once proceeded to do, ignoring the intervention of the numerous courtiers who surrounded the King and who, fearing for the safety of the Royal person, agitated for an immediate retreat across the Scheldt. One can imagine the Marshal delivering himself of a few well-chosen oaths and curses in their regard.

It was indeed to the credit of King Louis that he decided to ignore the mutterings of these weaker brethren and to remain on the battlefield. Saxe's subordinate, Lowendahl, of sterner stuff indeed, came up at the gallop from Roumignies, where he commanded part of the reserve, and requested permission to bring his troops into action, but the Marshal was already organising the first of a repeated series of counter-attacks. The first was delivered on the right of the British column by the Regiment du Roi, but this was driven off with some ease, although it was succeeded by a much more dangerous effort by several infantry units, including Royal Vaisseaux, Hainault, Soissonais and La Couronne. This, too, was flung back, however, by the deadly volleys of the Allied infantry.

Nevertheless, these attacks did, it seems, cause a partial withdrawal to a point close to the Fontenoy-

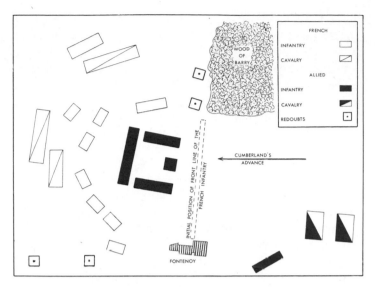

Map 3. The furthest advance. This map shows the area between the Wood of Barry and Fontenoy. Cumberland's infantry battalions have formed a species of square. In front are the French infantry remnants and the cavalry about to counter-attack

Wood of Barry line, where of course the troops came under the direct cross fire from the French artillery in the village and the redoubts. There followed some re-organisation, during which the entire force was formed into a species of large, hollow square, and it was again directed forward under Cumberland's guidance. Now, though, it was assailed by repeated cavalry charges, flung at them by Saxe while he prepared a single massive counter blow. These charges were not actually pressed home, that is, the horsemen did not come crashing full tilt into the infantry – this being a rare occurrence – but were rather rapid advances designed to cause the infantry to halt and prepare to receive the horsemen with levelled bayonets. To this end, regiment after regiment of French horse would ride boldly forward and then retire, all the while being fired at by the British infantry and sustaining damaging losses. Included in the charges were troops from the Maison du Roi, the King's

Household Cavalry, but they fared no better than their comrades of the line; of their units the Carabiniers in particular were roughly handled.

While this was taking place, and far to the left rear of the British infantry, the Dutch troops stood motionless. Saxe was calling up the rest of his reserves and bringing back into the fray some of the regiments already sorely battered in the first exchange of fire. Royal Vaisseaux, Hainault and Normandie regiments came back into line and were again decimated by the British musketry, although the latter were still under continuous fire from the French gun positions. Cumberland had for some time now realised that he was in mortal danger and had sent orders – it must have been a gallant messenger who carried them – to his cavalry standing uselessly far to the rear. At once they moved forward in compliance with the commander's instructions, but their intervention was too late, for by the time they had formed up and advanced they were thrown into confusion by a sudden rush to the rear of some Dutch and Austrian troops.

The crisis of the battle was now at hand, and it was about 1 o'clock. Saxe was ready to deliver his major counter attack. With this in view he moved forward his infantry line, backing it up with some of the best regiments he had still in hand, including the six battalions of the famous Irish Brigade – the Wild Geese – all of them burning with a desire to get to grips with their ancient enemies. The Normandie infantry came up as well, supported by the now rallied Gardes Françaises and Gardes Suisses, although it was not very likely that these units were in good shape after their demoralising experience of a few hours previously.

As Saxe said to his colleague Löwendahl, this was to be the final throw, the *coup de collier*, and having spoken thus, he signalled for the attack to be made. Eagerly the French and Irish infantry rushed forwards, cavalry coming up in support and many other units, shaken from previous fighting, also organised themselves to take part in the offensive action. Further to strengthen the attack Saxe ordered forward from behind Fontenoy where they were no longer required in view of the Dutch failure, two more infantry regiments – Piedmont and Crillon – but it appears they may have remained in their first positions, unwilling to move or misunderstanding their orders, something of an echo of Ingoldsby's conduct earlier in the day.

This all-out French attack was decisive, and it was made more so by the fortuitous bringing up to very close range of some cannon from a situation where they had seemingly been overlooked. The pressure on the allied square was tremendous, with cavalry making repeated advances and infantry pouring fire into the diminishing Allied ranks, until Cumberland, faced with imminent destruction, had no alternative but to order a retreat. The Irish Brigade had pushed their charge home and had crossed bayonets with the British, but had been held at bay with heavy losses. Nevertheless it was absolutely essential to save the still surviving forces, and 2 o'clock therefore saw the British and their allies in full retreat. It was a slow, completely disciplined and majestic progress, with frequent halts to turn about and deliver characteristic scorching volleys to keep the French cavalry at a distance. During the retrograde movement the British cavalry came forward and were able to hold up the French by partial charges, but despite this, the situation was dangerous in the extreme. Had the enemy decided upon a pursuit *à l'outrance*, it might well have gone badly for the Allied army and might even have resulted in something like a rout. This was not to be, however, and Saxe, by this time in a frightful physical condition with fatigue and the pain of his dropsy, did not order a pursuit, limiting French action to sending his Grassins to skirmish with the British rear guard. Thus Cumberland was able to reform his army behind Vezon and, reorganised to a very limited extent, to move off in retreat towards Ath.

The Battle of Fontenoy had been fought, lost and won.

8
Aftermath
of the Battle
◇◇◆◇◆◇◆

Painfully, the defeated allied army left the scene of battle, virtually without any interference from the French – a circumstance of which the enemies of Saxe did not fail to take advantage in their allegations that he deemed it to his own political and professional advantage to avoid inflicting total defeats on his foes, thus prolonging a war very beneficial to him personally. Be that as it may, the retreat was carried out more or less without incident, covered by a rearguard of Skelton's and Cholmondely's regiments (32nd and 34th Foot). To afford further protection the 3rd Foot (Buffs) were stationed in Vezon churchyard, screened and supported by the Black Watch, the whole being flanked by the British Cavalry. The field guns which had been man-handled forward by the infantry were perforce left behind and were gleefully seized by the French. It was later stated that a pair of colours had been captured by Bulkeley's Regiment of the Irish Brigade, these belonging to the Coldstream Guards. This is controversial, however, and up to the end of the last century the occurrence was still the subject of debate. It has for long been impossible to identify, through fading and inaccessibility of positioning in Les Invalides, many of the colours and standards captured by the French during the centuries, and the issue must still be considered an open one.

Having reformed beyond Vezon, Cumberland's forces marched to Ath, the thirteen miles involved being a severe strain, as the men were already at the limits of their powers after more than twelve hours spent under arms or in action. Fortunately, as we have said, there was no pursuit. Indeed it could well have been that Saxe's enemies misjudged in this instance, the Marshal's motives, or underestimated the difficulties of putting any sort of pursuit into operation, in the very confused and wooded terrain through which it would have taken place. There was also the fact that the very strong Dutch force – although, as we have seen, it was of no great fighting ability though certainly tremendously enthusiastic – was still in being and in theory could have launched an effective counter-attack against troops disorganised by a pursuit.

In any case, the French army had suffered very considerable casualties in the desperate fighting which had taken place, Fontenoy being one of the bloodiest battles of the century, exceeded in this respect only by some of the engagements fought by Frederick the Great.

The breakdown of Saxe's losses is as follows:

| Infantry officers | killed | 53 | wounded | 336 |
| Rank and file | killed | 1,662 | wounded | 3,110 |

In addition to the casualties in the infantry arm, the French cavalry had approximately 1,800 killed and wounded of all ranks, thus giving a total of very nearly 7,000.

The Allied losses, surprisingly enough, were only a fraction greater, although it must be recalled that the greatest part of these was suffered by the infantry battalions which had taken part in the push into the enemy's position and which had suffered so cruelly from the crossfire of artillery and musketry.

Details of the losses of certain British infantry regiments were thus:

	Killed	Wounded
Royal Welsh Fusiliers	189	322
Duroure's (12th)	159	321
Campbell's (21st)	5	286
Handasyde's (31st)	133	286
1st Guards	109	247
2nd Guards	114	239
3rd Guards	89	240

The losses in the Hanoverian infantry regiments were also heavy.

	Killed	Wounded
Böschlanger's	154	377
Zastrow's	90	299
Spören's	65	279
Oberg's	54	237
Campen's	67	210

Overall, cavalry losses in the Allied army were 168 killed and 483 wounded, the unit with the heaviest casualty list being the Royal Horse Guards. Through their supine behaviour on the left wing the Dutch lost relatively few men.

The defeat at Fontenoy was something of a shock for British public opinion although, not for the first nor the last time, largely by the accounts of the heroism of the troops engaged, a defeat was miraculously transformed into something – if not quite a victory – like a species of Dunkirk, with an attendant masochistic sort of glory. In practical terms, nevertheless, it was a catastrophe, for once Saxe had captured the fortress of Tournai, which he did in the June following, all Flanders fell to the

*Plate 1 Marshal Maurice de Saxe, victorious commander of the French
forces at Fontenoy. From the portrait by Latour*

Louis Quinze le Bien Aimé

Plate 2 Louis XV, king of France at the time of Fontenoy. From an engraving by Charles Parrocel

Plate 3 The Duke of Cumberland, Commander of the Allied army at the battle of Fontenoy. From the portrait by Morrier

Plate 4 Lieut.-General Jean-Louis Ligonier, Cumberland's General of Foot at Fontenoy. From the portrait by Reynolds

REFERENCES.
The English, Red.
Hanoverian, Yellow. Dutch, Orange.
Austrians, Green. French, Blue.
Here the French fled to their
Camp.
Afterwards we formed a Square
Battalion at Z, and retired in
good order to our Camp.

Plate 5 *The Allied plan of attack. Ligonier's infantry formed up at A,
and advanced against the French encampment, finally being forced to
form a square at Z prior to withdrawal under mounting French pressure.*
Reproduced by Gracious permission of Her Majesty the Queen

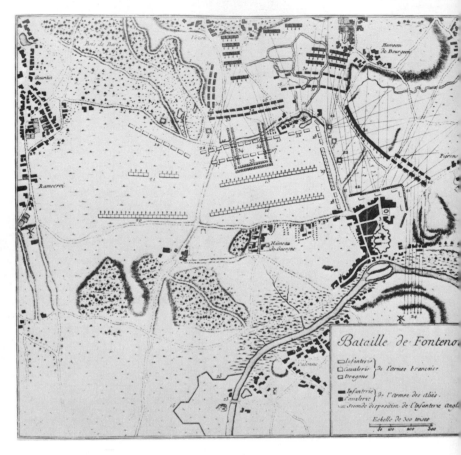

Plate 6 *A contemporary French map of the terrain and troop dispositions at Fontenoy. Compare with the map showing the battlefield from the English viewpoint*

Plate 7 *Awaiting the attack – the French Guards at Fontenoy. From a watercolour by Percy White (after Lalauze.)*

Plate 8 The French (foreground) and Allied armies face each other just before the climax of the battle. It was at this point that legend has it that Lord Charles Hay stepped forward from the ranks of the First Guards, saluted and drank a toast to the French, and then invited them to fire first!

French, and Cumberland was forced to retreat beyond Brussels in order to protect the all-important seaport of Antwerp. Other events were brewing at home, and soon there was to be equally serious and more pressing news to attract the attention both of the British people and its government.

Stories of a descent upon Scotland by the Jacobite 'Young Pretender' – Prince Charles Edward Stuart – were rife, and in this case Dame Rumour was far from being a lying jade. The Prince – although without the

Fig. 8. Trooper, Horse Guards (British)

promised French military assistance, which had really evaporated at Dunkirk the previous year – landed on the west coast of Scotland in July, 1745. Right speedily the Highlands were aflame. By September it was plain that a very serious revolt was in progress, and with Prince Charles and his army pressing forward towards Edinburgh, orders were sent for ten British battalions – the best available were to be selected – to be sent back immediately to England. So, in October, 1745, the leading elements of this force came ashore at Gravesend. The campaign of 1745 in the Low Countries was over with little or no success and with small profit other than to enhance the reputations of the regiments which had so bravely participated in the one great battle.

Militarily, Fontenoy has considerable tactical significance and serves dramatically to demonstrate that, when well placed in a carefully chosen defensive position, an army should have little difficulty in beating off an attack by any force of its own strength or less. Certainly it was particularly ill-advised to carry out anything like the frontal attack which was ordered – and to be fair to the man, led – by Cumberland. It remains but for us to attempt to assess the battle in the best possible way, that is by refighting it in miniature within the confines of a wargames table and within the framework of a body of rules applicable to the relevant period – that is, the middle years of the 18th Century.

We shall see what transpires.

9
Preparations
for the Wargame
◇◆◇◆◇◆◇◆◇◆◇

The Battle of Fontenoy has long held the greatest
fascination for me, both from the standpoint of the
student of history and from that of the wargamer, and
as long ago as 1964 I made an examination of the battle
in some depth, re-fighting every section of it separately
and in some cases in two different ways. Finally, the
results of the study were written up at some length in
the 'Special Issue' of *Wargamer's Newsletter* published
in the same year.

Being ten years ago, the rules employed for the playing
of the various wargames involved in the study were,
relatively speaking, in their infancy. Indeed, the course
of the examination itself – this really being its *raison
d'être* – revealed certain anomalies and inconsistencies,
which I did not hesitate to correct, so producing what
was to become – at least as far as I personally was concerned – a fairly definitive version of the Rules (those who
may be interested should consult *The War Game*,
published by A. and C. Black in 1971). Of course, continued research and examination of original sources over

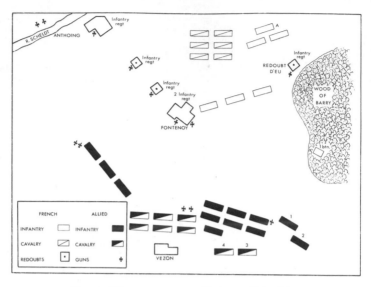

Map 4. The wargame : preliminary dispositions

the years have inevitably produced refinements, as doubtless they will continue to do. Nevertheless, the rules now detailed for the reconstitution of Fontenoy seem to me to give as close to an accurate simulation of the mid-18th Century battle as is compatible with accuracy of the representative firepower, fighting effect and movement rate, bearing in mind the inescapable fact that wargaming is, very properly, a game which must essentially be enjoyed by the participants.

With all this in view, we can proceed with the preliminary details for the setting up of the tabletop reconstitution of Fontenoy. First of all, although once again it would have been enlightening and enjoyable to have examined the fighting section by section – for example, by using the entire playing area to reproduce the ground between Fontenoy, the Wood of Barry and Vezon, or again, that between Fontenoy and Anthoing where the Dutch operated – it was decided that the entire battlefield should be transferred to the wargames table, so that the fighting could be done as a single

coherent whole. Or so was the pious hope at the start!
The terrain was accordingly set up as shown on Map
4. The table – and this is a particularly important consideration – was about the largest conveniently possible,
being an overall nine feet by seven. Anything larger
makes things difficult for all but the longest-armed
players, when fighting or movement takes place in the
central area – short of the players standing on chairs and
leaning perilously over the battlefield and its massed
fighting men, a larger size is impracticable! The area, of
course, should be sufficient to provide room for any
possible manoeuvre, but in view of our reconstruction,
it was decided that, although the players should have a
certain freedom of action, in general a better overall
picture of the action would result if the general course
of the battle was followed. This meant that operations
could take place on both sides of Fontenoy, with the
British/Hanoverian attack correlated with that of the
Dutch who, it was hoped, with a firm hand in command,
would make a more material contribution to the battle
than did their historical prototypes.

Actual terrain features were quite simple and consisted mainly of the forest area – the Wood of Barry –
together with the various villages, of which Fontenoy
and Anthoing were the principal ones. The River
Scheldt is shown in the top left corner, but only sufficient
of it to indicate its presence and to allow for the positioning of the French guns which enfiladed the left of the
Allied Army with, as we shall see, considerable effect.
One could write at considerable length about the theory
and practice of using wargame terrain features but
sufficient to say here that built-up areas – villages,
hamlets and the like – are indicated by an area of ground,
which is filled with the requisite number of miniature
buildings. These in turn are garrisoned, if so desired, by
the number of model soldiery representative of the
actual numbers of men who could, in real life, have
occupied such a built-up area. The same principles,
incidentally, apply to the redoubts raised to increase the

defensive value of the position held by the French.

Those between Fontenoy and Anthoing – actually three in number – can be seen to have been reduced to two, and the two on the far side of the Wood of Barry – from the Allied point of view, of course – are now but one, this of course being the famous (or infamous according to one's point of view!) Redoubt d'Eu. Much of the alteration of the actual terrain features – one can call it a species of juggling – need not have a basis in strict mathematics, but is largely inspired by the experience of the player setting the scene and his consequent 'feel' of the situation. Basically and simply, one must ensure that what has been transferred from map to table provides the essence of the tactical situation resulting from their presence. Certainly, as far as the Fontenoy–Anthoing front was concerned, two redoubts would, in the original battle, have been as effective as the original three, while on the other sector it was the single Redoubt d'Eu, or rather the fire therefrom – which in concert with that from Fontenoy did the damage to the Allied *masse de rupture*.

A further point concerns the various gradients or slopes, which were generally so slight as to be virtually imperceptible, the only one of any consequence being that which extended gently upwards from around Vezon to the ground between The Wood and Fontenoy. There is, however, no reason to cater for the reproduction of such an incline when its effect on the movement of troops is inappreciable, either to slow them down in an ascent or to impart any degree of impetus, say to a charge, when it was directed downhill. So, as this particular slope was by no means a steep one, certainly not enough to slow down the advance of Cumberland's battalions, it was deemed that for all practical purposes, it was level ground, and therefore in this area the table was uncluttered by any sloping or uneven ground. Of the natural features there remains only the Wood of Barry, which was shown generally by a line of model trees which indicated its circumference, together with a few groups in the middle to illustrate that it was, in fact, a continuous wooded area. Now, obviously, had it been so desired for aesthetic or other purpose to show a solid area of trees, this could well have been done, but such a representation has disadvantages when it comes to moving miniature soldiery through it. Players' fingers get caught in the branches, figures become tangled in the foliage and general confusion and irritation tend to develop. One has but to ensure that, in a forest or wood indicated only by a circumference of trees, the movement of troops therein is governed by the laws limiting ordinary speed in such conditions and that visibility is also appropriately curtailed for troops operating in the wood. This, of course, is a choice the wargamer has to make, but I submit that should the tactical necessities be provided for, all then is well with the 'circumference system'.

The question of the man-made terrain features – fortifications and redoubts – is easily answered. Earthworks were essentially heaped-up soil reinforced by roughly hewn wooden beams and tree trunks, and simply formed a chest-high protection, a species of elevated trench, affording a firing platform for the muskets of the defending infantry, while here and there the continuous line would be pierced with large apertures to allow any guns sited there a satisfactory field of fire. They can be of fairly elaborate construction, wargamewise, but on the other hand need only be totally functional: lengths of balsa wood glued together to form a triangular section, vertical on the side of the defenders, sloping towards the enemy and of sufficient height to reach to the chest of a wargame infantryman. Painted in some brown or earth colour, they provide adequate reproductions of the redoubts set up by Marshal Saxe. Square, and some 6″ per side, they will be capable of accommodating an appropriate number of infantry representative of the real-life garrisons of the redoubts as they were organised by the Marshal.

Now that we have mentioned the numbers of troops – that is, the actual model soldiers employed – it might be timely to say something about them. It seems fair to say that the most popular size of a miniature for wargaming is nowadays the 25 mm., i.e. the infantry soldier is 25 mm. in height without headgear, while the cavalryman is correspondingly larger. Without wishing to complicate matters overmuch it should be pointed out that the actual size of the miniatures is not a hundred per cent important. What is vital, however, is the ground scale, this being the relationship between distance on the table and that on the real battlefield, for upon this the size of wargame units and consequently that of armies is based. Let us suppose, for the sake of example, that we take the scale as being $1'' = 10$ yards. All movements and ranges as well as unit strengths are based on this.

To give just one instance, let us consider an infantry battalion drawn up in line, three ranks deep, in what was termed 'close order for firing'. Taking it as having an average strength on active service as some 600 men, and allowing them the correct spacing, not quite shoulder to shoulder, it would cover a frontage of some 120 yards, this giving us, in our chosen scale, a table equivalent of $12''$. If this distance is occupied by troops – the miniature variety of course – then what we have is a wargame battalion, irrespective of the size of figure and the numbers involved. Naturally, both for accuracy and appearance (the latter being a far from unimportant consideration), the more actual figures there are, the greater the degree of verisimilitude there will be, and by this token 25 mm. will be found to be most acceptable. This will be marginally less so for the once popular 30 mm. figure, while the old 'toy soldier' size – the 54 mm. – will be much too large. With the first – the 25 mm. – the $12''$ of the battalion frontage will be occupied by up to 24 or 25 figures, in sharp contrast to the half dozen or so of the largest type we have mentioned. Of course, it is not a matter of mere numbers only, but of units which can be fitted into the area they occupied in the actual battle, so that when the wargame which purports to trace its progress is being played it is most essential that these will have the tactical effect on the table as did their prototypes on the historic battlefield. 'Scaling down' and 'juggling' are two of the words which spring quickly to mind in this context, and both will have to be brought into operation as we set about deploying our armies, to give them as far as possible the effect their real life counterparts enjoyed a couple of centuries ago. Possibly I may be forgiven a little repetition if I say that this is a matter of experience and for want of a better phrase, having the 'feel' of the situation.

There is, in fact, no need to enter too deeply into the mechanics of how one converts 50,000 actual troops into their wargame equivalent. It is really sufficient to say that what results when the conversion is made should be comparable strengths, organised in units – regiments, battalions or what you will – which individually or *en bloc* are able to manoeuvre and operate as their man-size equivalents were able to do. Thus, before proceeding further, let me say a few very brief words on the wargame organisation which experience has shown to afford a most excellent simulation of mid-18th Century military practice, taking the infantry regiment as an example. In my own organisation (and this is as used in the Battle of Fontenoy) an infantry regiment numbers 48 rank and file, with five officers. The latter are the colonel – mounted, naturally – a colour-bearer or ensign, and three subaltern officers, this making a total therefore of 53 actual wargame figures. In the 1″ to 10 yards scale already discussed, this would in fact equate with the customary infantry battalion of some 600 men. (The fact that I call it a 'regiment' is neither here nor there and is simply a matter of nomenclature.)

So, a quick reference to the map of the preliminary wargame dispositions reveals that the Allied infantry numbered twelve regiments, while there were eight of cavalry. At the same time the French had twelve regiments of infantry and six of cavalry, together with an additional battalion, this being the light infantry – the Grassins – numbering 3 officers and 24 men. Artillery was similarly scaled down, Saxe disposing of eight cannon, while the Allies had six only.

I think it only fair at this stage to point out that the normal $1'' = 10$ yards scale really has to be abandoned in a reconstruction battle such as we are undertaking, where the table has to represent a much greater area than can be coped with by adhering to the $1'' = 10$ yards scale. It must be emphasised that not only does the ground scale govern the representative strength of a battalion or other unit, but also the time occupied by the 'moves' or 'periods' into which a wargame is divided. Let me explain. In the time occupied by a normal 'move' or 'period' an infantry unit – taking this as a simple example – can advance $6''$ (or 60 yards, whichever concept is preferred), this being the customary marching pace of the time, in effect 60 yards per minute. This is fine for the true game scale; it is otherwise where space has been pretty ruthlessly compressed. Here, instead of the 'period' allowing movement of $6''$ (or 6 yards) it would in fact be much greater than this.

Indeed, examining the map of the actual battle which we transferred to the table, we find that the $6''$ equals not 60 yards but something like 420 yards. Thus, in consequence, when infantry moves $6''$ the time occupied is not one minute but something like seven. Allowing for halts, the time taken up with the communication of orders, dressing and deploying, it may even be ten minutes, or possibly more.

This explanation of the time factor should answer the potential question as to how a major battle such as this can be completed in, possibly, a score of wargame periods – or twenty minutes of real time. By taking the time as being determined by the move, it would be something like 200 minutes – getting on for $3\frac{1}{2}$ hours in fact, a much more realistic time for such an engagement to run its course. As we shall see in due course, this extension of time will, among other things, make far more realistic the long and painful advance carried out by Cumberland's infantry into the very heart of the enemy position.

In the same way, one of the infantry regiments which in normal scale represents a battalion will be found, in this enlarged version, to be in fact approximately the equal of an entire brigade, and we shall see almost immediately how our units will 'double' for much larger formations.

We shall now – and, after this lengthy preamble, not before time – proceed to set out the actual wargame troops and indicate how they were disposed. To this end certain consultations took place with the participants – the 'generals', in fact – as to just what stage of the proceedings they wished to have laid out. It was decided that the starting point should be roughly about the time when Cumberland had arrayed his forces preparatory to making the right flank move against the Wood of Barry. In all this those organising the proceedings had to be more than a little careful, for there is one thing which must always be in the mind of wargamers re-enacting an historic battle – too much advantage from 'hindsight' should be allowed. After all knowing from his history what took place, no wargamer in his right mind would have persisted in the course followed by Cumberland, above all were the battle being fought within the framework of a campaign.

In any event, starting first with the Allied army, the main striking force was deployed to make a really serious attempt on the French left, as of course Cumberland did. This was really a pretty logical proceeding, as all were very aware of the deadliness of the flanking artillery fire from the guns across the Scheldt which would have to be sustained by troops massed on the Allied left and making any movement towards the Anthoing sector. Seven regiments of infantry made up this force deployed in front of Vezon, three in each of the two front lines and one only in the third. This seemed to be a fairly reasonable reproduction of Cumberland's dispositions and in this arrangement we actually do see our single infantry regiment representing an historical infantry brigade.

To the right of this mass – the British and Hanoverian

infantry – and positioned slightly *en potence* were two more regiments. This was a higher relative proportion than was Ingoldsby's task force, but it was considered, not unreasonably, that, appreciating the power of the defensive position afforded by the Wood of Barry, a sensible general would have designated a stronger force to face it than did Cumberland. Three regiments only represented the Dutch infantry, their task being merely to mask the right face of the French 'L' and to prevent, if possible, troops from the Anthoing–Fontenoy sector being withdrawn to support the French left wing. The eight regiments of Allied cavalry were positioned as shown, six to the left of the main infantry concentration and directly in front of Vezon, with two in immediate support of Cumberland's infantry. Five actual guns represented the Allied artillery, two to the left of the Dutch and protecting their left flank and two and one on the left and right of Cumberland respectively. The light guns which were manhandled forwards by the advancing infantry were ignored, as contributing only slightly to the overall effect of the combined British and Hanoverian musketry.

On the French side, 'Marshal Saxe' drew out his army very much as did his illustrious predecessor. One regiment of infantry (again the 5 officers, 48 rank and file composition) was stationed in Anthoing, with one each in the two redoubts between that place and Fontenoy, which itself held two more regiments. Prolonging the line, three regiments held the ground between Fontenoy and the Redoubt d'Eu, which was occupied by a single similar regiment. Three regiments – two being the Dillon and Bulkeley 'Wild Geese' units – were deployed as a reserve in the position shown and the six cavalry regiment were massed to the rear. Two of the French guns were in position beyond the River Scheldt, with one each in Anthoing and the two redoubts between there and Fontenoy, which itself had two. The eighth and last was in the Redoubt d'Eu. It was considered unnecessary to make any actual disposition for the troops across the Scheldt as they were unlikely to have had any effect on the action.

Finally we note that the lower end of the Wood of Barry is occupied by a single battalion of infantry, this being the redoubtable Arquebussiers de Grassin. It is probably unnecessary to point out, as really being obvious, that infantry of the line, trained to move and fire in close order formations, are very much at a disadvantage in woods vis-a-vis light infantry (such as the Grassins) whose natural habitat and favourite theatre of operations this type of country provides. Consequently wargame rules should properly give them powers rather in excess of those of the line, who under normal circumstances would sweep them away with some ease in the open field. However, we shall see, without labouring the point, just how light infantry fare against attack by the brothers of the line – and as two Allied regiments are plainly deployed for this purpose, we shall not have long to wait.

10
Something about the Imponderable
◆◇◆◇◆◇◆◇◆◇◆

With our wargame troops in position and poised for action it might be a good thing were we to make a few further general points concerning wargame rules, and how they apply to the particular battle we are ready and eager to fight. This will concern the principles of wargaming, and more especially the manner in which we simulate the uncertainty of military operations. While normally one can assess the probability of some operation following a planned and predictable course, the hoped-for or anticipated result is never an absolute certainty. In effect, the difference can be most graphically described by a comparison with the game of chess, in itself a most ancient form of the wargame, although highly stylised and mathematical.

In chess, if one wants to move, say, a bishop from one square to another, one simply picks up the piece and deposits it in the desired position. In wargaming, on the contrary, if a 'general' – the player, that is – desires a certain unit to move from Point 'A' to Point 'B' and issues orders to this effect, circumstances may show that the unit does nothing of the kind, or will even act quite at variance with the player's wishes. In such a case, we have reached the point where the player is no longer fully in command of the unit, as a chess player is always in control of his piece. This sort of thing reproduces exactly the situation where a commander issues an order and the subordinate who receives it fails to understand its import or just refuses to carry it out. Such an occurrence is but one instance of how nothing is absolutely certain in war, and real-life examples of such a happening are not hard to find, one classic example being that of the cavalry at the Battle of Minden (1759) when the commander, Lord George Sackville, simply refused to comply with repeated orders from his commanding general to charge with his horsemen. While always possible, such an event is such an unpredictable thing that there is no means of coping with it other than by bringing in a factor of uncertainty which we shall have to consider at all times. It is, in fact, a species of variable or imponderable, consisting of the effect of circumstances and of all kinds of contributory influences, physical and psychological, which can effect the actions of a man or a group of men.

Let me illustrate what may be a fairly obscure point with a single example. In pursuance of its orders, a unit of infantry is marching happily along a valley to a destination at its further end when it is suddenly taken aback by the unexpected appearance upon the surrounding hills of masses of enemy troops all filled with much malice aforethought, and ready to smite the infantry unit hip and thigh. What does the latter do, in such a case? Does it carry out its orders, does it halt in confusion, or does it even turn tail and run? This will depend upon a veritable multiplicity of conditions – how well trained and disciplined it is; how fatigued or how fresh it might be; on how many enemy can be seen and whether any friendly support is at hand; and on the quality of its officers and how confident the men are of their qualities of leadership. These are the visible and material factors, it can be said, but to them must be added the totally unpredictable one, that which reflects the fact that it is never certain – as we have been at pains to stress – how a group of men under stress will behave in any given situation. To illustrate this, military history amply demonstrates that sometimes even a highly disciplined or 'crack' regiment can behave like a mob of raw recruits, or conversely, how, on occasion, a raw and poorly trained unit will fight like demons. It is in such circumstances, for example when a regiment first comes under fire in a battle, or is surprised, or indeed finds itself in any of the many situations wherein its morale is subject to an unusual amount of pressure, that we have to determine just what its reaction will be.

In the wargame this is not, and need not be, a complicated procedure. One uses a combination of the facts of the case such as we have shown above as an example, together with an 'imponderable' – a portentous word, but I can really think of none which better fits the case – to determine, with reference to previously prepared probability charts, what the reaction is likely to be. The imponderable is really such a thing of 'luck', of 'fortune', that it is quite simply assessed by some sort of dice throw, between one and three of these essential objects being employed, depending upon the wargame rules in use. This, plus all the physical circumstances relative to the case, will determine whether the unit's reaction is favourable or otherwise. The charts referred to are so prepared that normally a well-trained and seasoned unit will obey its orders, unless the circumstances are frantically against it. They – the charts – are also so designed that, unless lucky, a hastily recruited, 'green' battalion – say one of militia, possibly – is much more likely to shirk the issue, should there be one, or fail to come up to expectations. Provisions are built in for the exceptional case, of course, but these will normally be rare, and if a unit – of whatever quality – is under very severe pressure, has lost many officers, and is facing heavy odds, the chances favour its morale failure.

If a wargamer looks after his troops properly, with due regard to the art and craft of warfare – making sure, for instance, that he never leaves a regiment completely unsupported, that it always has at least potential flank cover, and that it is not unnecessarily fatigued (yes, indeed, this can readily be catered for in the wargame) – then it will generally obey its orders as far as possible. The exception will be if the highly unlikely or near-impossible situation develops, as it can in each and every form of human activity of endeavour. So, all being well, unlucky dice throwing – to resolve the imponderable – should never be solely responsible for the bad behaviour of a unit – or at least this should not take place if the wargame rules are realistic and properly balanced.

In a way, the same idea applies to the fire power of infantry, or indeed any sort of missile fire. The system may best be explained thus. When one body of infantry fires at another – in whatever period or with whatever weapon – two extremes of possibility present themselves. On the one hand, every single musket – or whatever – can miss its target, or at the opposing end of the spectrum, every shot can take effect. Now, both extremes will obviously be of unbelievable rarity, and practice, experience and experiment (the last with unit-sized canvas targets) through the many years during which the smooth bore musket was operational, provided ample evidence that there was always a consistently average number of hits – a 'norm' – round which the variation up or down, in terms of the number of hits, was comparatively small.

Knowing such figures and the normal amount of variation, we can proceed to postulate that, at certain ranges, a unit had a certain definite effect when firing at another, this being a sort of 'mean'. It is this 'mean' we use in the wargame to determine the effect of musketry on various types of target troops. When Battalion 'A' fires at Battalion 'B', for example, 'x' casualties are ordinarily inflicted, but this can vary slightly, and we simulate this by having recourse to our old friends the dice, the throw of which may show that the casualties are indeed 'x–y', the latter being a relatively small number. If, let us suppose, the norm were 18 – that is to say 18 casualties were inflicted, a ' $-y$ ' would give a deduction of 3, and a ' $+y$ ' an addition of the same number. This is merely a random example and again serves to show that the use of the dice is strictly limited and that they provide merely a convenient means of helping to create the small variation which tends to take the wargame out of the purely mathematical into something which we hope reproduces an indication of the uncertainty of war in all its aspects.

A similar procedure operates for the occasions when hand-to-hand fighting or mêlée occurs, whereby weight is given to the better class of soldiery – the elite troops – as well as advantage to those with the impetus provided by their charging as against those who may be standing fast, or troops coming downhill, to give another example. Cannon fire of various kinds – roundshot, shell or canister – is also partially governed by the use of the imponderable. My personal inclination is for the use of various forms of visual device, whereby the fall of shell, the path of a cannon ball, or the 'spread' of a round of canister are shown by patterns or templates, superimposed on the target, and with casualties inflicted in correct proportion to the probability of hits. The element of chance again enters into our calculations, but again it operates solely within the framework of the established 'mean' or 'norm'.

It is obvious that in these notes it is impossible to give anything other than a very limited account of how such rules operate and how they are derived. Books have been written on the subject – the writer pleads guilty to having done so himself – but this chapter will afford some indication as to the principles of what we are about to carry out – which is, of course, a serious attempt to recreate within the confines of a wargame table, the action and conditions prevailing in a military action in the year 1745.

11
The Wargame

And so, let battle finally commence.

Naturally, 'Marshal Saxe', with the defensive tactics of his prototype very much in his mind, was obviously prepared to play a waiting game, and during the first two or three periods of the action contented himself with closely observing his enemy's movements, at the same time venturing a few bursts of roundshot from his guns at Fontenoy village, these being within range of the Allied masses in front of Vezon, as well as the Dutch troops on the other side of the same village. These shots resulted in minimal effect and were deemed by 'Cumberland' to be 'frighteners' only. Initially, however, this selfsame individual seemed rather reluctant to move forward, and it seemed that with the formidable obstacle of the Wood of Barry threatening the flank of the advance he was about to make, he had decided to clear it completely, or at the very least to neutralise the marksmen lurking in its depths.

To this end, then, his right hand brigade – Regiments 1 and 2 – deployed into line (two deep being the maximum deployment at which all muskets may be discharged) and advanced towards the edge of the wood, immediately coming under long range fire from the Grassins, who had now moved in considerable numbers right up to the fringe of trees. At first, as it was at too great a range for the light infantry to concentrate their attentions on the officers of the attacking units – by picking them off – they fired 'into the brown', causing some casualties, although not as many as 'Saxe' would have liked, and the steady advance of the infantry continued. Very wisely, they held their fire, hoping to get in their first – and naturally their most effective – volley at as close a range as possible.

As the two Allied regiments drew nearer, 'Saxe', from his position at Fontenoy, was a most interested spectator, and, apparently coming to the conclusion that the threat posed to his position in the wood was rather more considerable than could be dealt with by the battalion of Grassins (outnumbered by more than four to one by the Allied infantry approaching them), he ordered one of his reserve infantry regiments to move into the Wood. This was Regiment 'A' – the Grenadiers de Penthievre – its entry into the wood leaving only the two regiments of the Irish Brigade – Bulkeley and Dillon – in reserve beyond the Redoubt d'Eu.

By this time, the Allied infantry brigade had come to a point where they were in very close proximity to the edge of the Wood, and heavier losses than they had suffered in their approach were now being inflicted upon them. However, in the fourth period of the game, on coming into close range (in wargame terms, 6″) they delivered their first volley. This, with muskets being carefully loaded in camp under the supervision of sergeants and not being subject to the errors commonly resulting from the heat and pressure of battle, is ordinarily expected to be more deadly than its successors. In this case, though, the Grassins did enjoy the partial cover afforded by the trees, behind which they were positioned, and the volley was not perhaps as effective as it might have been. Although a number of casualties were inflicted, a resulting test of the Grassins' morale – this must be done whenever a unit has suffered casualties – showed that it was still satisfactory, despite their fairly isolated position.

The Grenadiers de Penthievre had just entered the Wood and were some considerable distance away. In any event, it was evident to the 'French' that the Grassins could not be expected to hold their current advanced position against a really strong and determined advance and they gradually began to withdraw back through the Wood, into which the British regiments plunged in pursuit. This at once put the latter at a fairly severe disadvantage, as line infantry have to break formation when moving through forested or wooded areas. Consequently, being no longer able to bring their close order musketry into action, their firing is therefore far from being as effective as it is in the open. Of course, by the same token, the fire of the defending light infantrymen was reduced in range – because of the density of the trees, naturally – but, *being* light infantry, they were now, man for man, considerably more effective than the line infantry, although still seriously outnumbered.

On period five, then, with the disappearance of his right flanking infantry brigade into the Wood of Barry, and with the Grassins removed from his ken for the time being, 'Cumberland', now deeming it appropriate to move, set his ponderous masses into action – the seven regiments of his striking force advancing steadily and directly forward (following historical precedent), the flanking artillery, which had not unlimbered, initially moving forward along with the infantry. At the same time, and possibly as a kind of diversion to create some doubt in the French mind – and possibly even to cause 'Saxe' to consider the possibility of an attack on his right, four of the Allied cavalry regiments were moved to their left, with the apparent intention of joining the Dutch infantry as a prelude to a possible attack.

This move did not, however, succeed in deceiving the

French 'Marshal', and he did not evince any concern about his right flank during the entire battle. Indeed, as the Dutch infantry also shifted its position leftwards and slightly closer to the Scheldt, he was able to bring his guns beyond that river into action causing no little trouble to the Dutch, the roundshot enfilading their lines instead of plunging through from front to rear of shallow formations. Again, with their first casualties, the Dutch were obliged to have a test of their morale. They were found to be in good heart and 'Cumberland' was, for the time being, able to breathe more freely.

As the Allied line infantry in the wood could move at only half their normal speed, their comrades in the main force before long reached a position where they were abreast to them, and in consequence some of the Grassins were able to sidestep to their right, appear on the edge of the wood and fire from there. They were insufficient in numbers, however, to do much damage in this quarter, their main body being more than fully occupied with the steady progress of the two Allied regiments which had penetrated the Wood. Rather more severe, though, was the increasing effect of the French cannon, which now began to inflict heavier losses on 'Cumberland's' advancing seven regiments than he was really happy about. He therefore halted his troops.

This was now period seven, which he occupied in unlimbering his three pieces of artillery preparatory to engaging in some counter-battery fire with the French guns. This was something of an error, for counter-battery fire is never an unqualified success (indeed, in later years, no less a personage than the Duke of Wellington chided, in somewhat salty terms, an artillery officer he found directing fire at enemy guns). It was, in the days of which we speak, generally far easier and more profitable to aim one's guns at enemy infantry masses, rather than to fire in the hope of hitting an enemy field piece in a vital spot – a tiny and very difficult target without a doubt. However, 'Cumberland' did not take long to perceive his mistake, although he wasted several

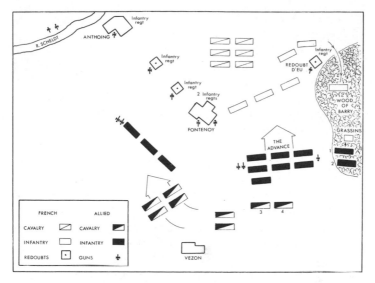

Map 5. Situation at end of period 9

precious periods of play (it takes a complete period to unlimber a gun, and the same time to limber it up). As quickly as possible he moved on his infantry without waiting for his guns to limber up. They, perforce, had to follow on behind as soon as they were able.

Meanwhile, the two cavalry regiments – 3 and 4 – which had originally been deployed to the rear of the infantry, had also moved forward, but were some way to the rear of the main infantry mass. All this time there had been no move by any of 'Saxe's' troops, save, that is, the entry of the Penthievre Regiment into the wood. At the end of Period 9 the situation is as shown on Map 5. So far, there had not been a great deal of action – certainly nothing dramatic – but tension was mounting rapidly – let no one claim there is any lack of tension round a wargame table – and throughout the game had been carried out in a most pregnant silence.

By period 9, however, the 'crunch' was rapidly approaching. In the Wood of Barry part of the Grassins had lingered overlong in their sniping at the approaching

Allied infantry and had been caught by them in a hand-to-hand fight, losing several of their number in the process. The infantry had nevertheless suffered considerable losses, particularly among their officers, as, with the closing range, the Grassins had been able to pick them off, a more difficult thing to accomplish – wargamewise – than firing into the brown, and very valuable when as assessment of morale has to be made. Obviously, the fewer the surviving officers, the less strong will be the control or command element and the more likely it will be for a unit so deprived to fail in its mission, to halt in indecision, or even – horror of horrors! – to break and run.

Fortunately for the Allied troops pushing through the wood, such tests of morale had been uniformly satisfactory, but there had been one bad moment when the figure representing the general commanding the brigade – a local substitute for the egregious Ingoldsby – had been hit. It was but a superficial wound – this being established by a dice throw – and he was able to continue in command. Having been caught in hand-to-hand combat as we have seen, the Grassins had been handled pretty roughly overall and their numbers – 3 officers and 24 men to begin with – had been somewhat depleted. Their morale, however, remained good in spite of their losses. Still, the visage of 'Cumberland', when it peered in this direction betrayed unmistakable signs of satisfaction.

Less agreeable thoughts must have filled his mind, though, when he contemplated the progress of his main column, which was now coming under a truly deadly crossfire – albeit at extreme range – of canister from the guns in Fontenoy and the single piece in the Redoubt d'Eu. 'Saxe', seeing that there was no apparent or immediate danger to his right wing, had already moved the right hand gun in Fontenoy to the other side of the village, in which direction danger more urgently threatened. The concentrated fire from the two guns in battery made steady inroads into the strengths of the seven Allied regiments, although yet again, things could have been worse. Certain adjustments in the French infantry line were now seen to be in operation, the Gardes Françaises and the Gardes Suisses drawing more closely together, while both regiments of the Irish Brigade moved to their right, directly behind the three front line regiments. At the same time, from the Redoubt d'Eu there emerged its garrison – Soissonais Infantry – which moved at once into the wood where, considerably further away, the Penthievre regiment was preparing to succour the Grassins, now in full retreat before the triumphant Allied infantry.

Deeming that the moment of truth was now imminent, the Dutch infantry began a fairly cautious advance, directing themselves towards the space between Fontenoy and the nearest redoubt on the Anthoing side, and coming under immediate and continuous fire from their front and also from the guns beyond the Scheldt. Despite this, their morale continued to be satisfactory. Simultaneously, the leading regiments in the main Allied force came into extreme range of the French main line muskets. No time was wasted by the Gardes Françaises and the other two units, who all fired at once, hoping to be able to deliver at least a couple of volleys as their opponents closed up to them. The first volley did little damage and 'Cumberland', true to history, did not allow his troops to fire but kept them steadily advancing.

A lively little action was taking place in the Wood of Barry, where the Grenadiers de Penthievre closed with the leading British infantry regiment. There was a fierce struggle, at the end of which the French, having been able to bring more men into the combat than the British, drove the latter back, although the second Allied regiment was deployed a little to the rear, ready to receive the French as they pressed through the wood.

Rather surprisingly, on the further side of Fontenoy village, possibly assisted by the earlier withdrawal of the gun by 'Saxe', the first Dutch infantry regiment, moving in column and thereby advancing more rapidly than the

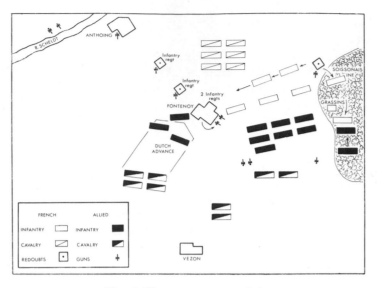

Map 6. The wargame on period 13

main force which was in line, had reached the breastworks round the village and were actually in hand-to-
hand combat with the defenders. The following Dutch
regiments, however, had crowded in behind their leader
and were consequently in some confusion. So, with the
Dutch actually engaged with the French, the situation
in Period 13 was as depicted on Map 6.

Already signs of strain were visible, and the left-hand
regiment of 'Cumberland's' front line had suffered so
severely – the Colonel and two officers had fallen as well
as many rank and file – that a test of its morale showed
that it would have to retire behind its support, there to
reorganise as quickly as it could. This was expedited by
one of 'Cumberland's' senior Aides-de-camp – as is
permitted by the rules – taking over the command. This
procedure naturally takes some little time – a complete
wargame period, in fact – during which the unit involved
is ineffective. Still, the Allies were now in close enough
proximity to the French for them to attempt to repeat the
devastating first volley of the historical battle. This they

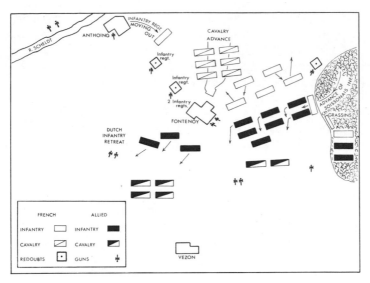

Map 7. Period 15 – beginning of the end

proceeded to do, splendidly, but without the complete success their prototypes had enjoyed. Two of the French regiments, certainly, were shattered and indeed fled, but the third, the Gardes Françaises, stood fast in the centre of the extremely depleted line.

However, the day was really saved for 'Saxe' by the appearance on the Allied right flank – coming suddenly into sight on the edge of the wood – of the infantry regiment which had been cleverly brought from the Redoubt d'Eu and moved through the Wood of Barry into this position, whence they fell upon the right flank unit of the Allied front line, the First Guards. This rude and sudden stroke was understandably too much for this regiment – an unexpected flank attack invariably being fatal in most circumstances for the recipient – and it was tumbled back in ruins into the second rank of the mass. Wisely, Soissonais forebore to pursue, but stood its ground, pouring musketry into the Allied ranks.

'Cumberland' was now unmistakably in a very great dilemma. The places of the broken French regiments had been taken by the two Irish Brigade regiments and they and the Gardes Françaises were now exchanging fire with the Allies, while all the time the guns on the flanks were pouring rounds of canister into 'Cumberland's' ranks. The two cavalry regiments which had been in the rear had moved up in support but could not get close enough to drive off the Soissonais regiment, and were themselves coming under scattered fire from the remnants of the Grassins, again lining the edge of the Wood of Barry.

The Dutch regiment assailing the village of Fontenoy had, with some assistance, actually penetrated the breastworks at one point but had been flung out. Their supporting units had suffered too much from artillery fire to renew the assault while a morale test showed that the one which had actually pressed home the attack was obliged to fall back to reorganise. Far beyond the French infantry line, now again firmly established in their original positions, 'Saxe's' cavalry was beginning to move forward, and it was evident that a powerful counter-attack was in course of preparation. Further misfortune was in store, as the centre Allied infantry unit – the Coldstream Guards – had now, through heavy losses, to have a morale check. With several officers lost and over a quarter of the rank and file casualties it was not surprising that it, too, had to fall back to the rear of the second line. In the Wood of Barry itself there seemed to be a species of stalemate, with the Soissonais holding the Allies at arm's length and engaging in desultory musketry.

Assessing the situation, then, 'Cumberland' really had no alternative. It would have been extremely unwise to attempt another advance against the French with three out of his seven regiments very badly shaken and all having suffered substantial losses. It did not seem possible to bring his rather scattered cavalry together to make an attack, and indeed against such a position it would have been the height of folly. The infantry regiment which had been positioned in Anthoing had now also been brought forward and there was the very strong possibility that it and the French cavalry would be launched in an attack, either against the left or right wings of the Allied army, so, all things being considered, 'Cumberland' had no choice but to order a retreat. Accordingly, all his regiments began to move to the rear, with the French following up steadily and firing at the retiring units. On the 18th period they halted, this being considered the end of the day's fighting. (What constitutes a day in wargame terms is subject to numerous interpretations, but in such a battle as that whose progress we have described, the number of periods given is taken as representing the amount of time which would actually have been positively occupied with military action, allowing for inevitable delays in transmission, reception and digestion of orders, and so on.)

It was assumed that 'Saxe' followed historical precedent in declining to carry out a pursuit *à l'outrance*, but there is no doubt that his victory was a complete one, with 'Cumberland' well and truly trounced, as the actual details will reveal in the next chapter.

12
Analysis
of the Game

◇◆◇◆◇◆◇◆◇

The factor which must be initially considered in the process of analysis of our wargame is probably a simple statement of the losses which the two sides suffered, to establish in what degree they relate to those suffered by the combatants in the historical battle. At this stage it may be proper to point out that when, as a result of enemy action on the wargames table, casualties have been inflicted on one's units and figures have accordingly been removed from the scene of operations, they do not necessarily represent the actual slain but simply those who have been rendered *hors-de-combat*, even though this may be as the result of only slight wounds.

In point of fact, in a wargame which is part of an overall campaign, due consideration must be given to the various important factors of transport, of the recruiting and replacement of troops, to the availability of medical services and so on. Accordingly, where the battle which has been fought is not an isolated encounter *in vacuo*, but one which has a place in a pattern of warfare, and where it is important for a player to extricate from a lost battle as much as he can in the way of men and material in order to prepare for a subsequent and possibly more successful encounter, then it is important to decide what proportion of the immediate battle losses are permanent and which are but temporary. In such battles, wounded can be carried off by transport provided for the purpose, to be delivered to hospitals to be rendered fit to fight another day, and even a general may be helped on his way by comrades. In such cases it has to be decided by precedent how long such wounded will be deemed to be incapacitated.

It can be approximately established from historical records just what proportion of the wounded in the battles of the period with which we are concerned was likely to recover and what proportion, by reason of the severity of their wounds, was totally out of action for the remainder of the campaign. Alas, medical science in the 18th Century – and this especially applies when we think of the rough and ready systems operating in what, with some stretch of the imagination, may be called field hospitals – was not sufficiently advanced to save many whose recovery would have been ensured by later techniques. Thus although there were considerable variations in the ratio due to conditions of climate, speed of arrival and extent of the medical assistance, we can take it that something like a quarter of the total casualties in a battle were killed or mortally wounded, and that the bulk of the remainder would at some later date be able to return to their places in the ranks. It is stressed that these figures are to some degree speculative as records upon which they are based are incomplete and fragmentary, so the proportions given are open to some doubt. In any case, this all leads up to the fact that what we shall consider in our Battle of Fontenoy is a sum of all the casualties, the dead and the mortally wounded, and those temporarily out of action, some of the latter category being theoretically able to rejoin their units as early as the following day, so that only a quarter need be considered as 'killed'.

With this in mind, let us first look at the battle casualties in wargame figures, bearing in mind that we are now dealing with the present-day highly sophisticated type of wargame in contrast to that of yesteryear when, before the advent of the very realistic type of rules now generally in use, a wargame was quite likely to terminate unequivocally with about half a dozen figures left standing in the ranks of the winner's army and possibly none at all in those of the loser – happily, such things went out with the firing of matches from miniature cannon! So, referring to our figures, we find that on the Allied side 109 British and 31 Dutch figures were removed – the former almost entirely from the regiments which took part in the perilous march up to the French position – and that 14 cavalry figures were also lost. On the side of 'Saxe', 126 infantry figures were lost and no cavalry whatsoever, the former again being largely from the first line of infantry, although in the course of the prolonged fighting in the Wood of Barry, the Grassins lost almost half their strength, a very heavy casualty list for a small unit.

Comparing the infantry losses, then – those of the cavalry being relatively minimal – we find by a little calculation that Allied infantry losses amounted to just over 20% and that of the French infantry just under that proportion. Now, taking into account the cavalry casualties, we find that, in round figures, the Allies suffered an overall loss of some 16% and the French about 15%. These are a trifle larger than those we have earlier noted as having been incurred in the actual battle, but the latter may well have included the very lightly wounded who 'fell in' as soon as their regiments rallied. In any case, a comparison of the actual and the wargame totals show that they are sufficiently close to have given a most satisfying degree of authenticity and verisimilitude to the game, from the point of view of the players and of those who organised it.

I hasten to add that such figures are very far from being the be-all and the end-all, for what is far more important in our examination of the battle is whether – and this is not too easy to describe in clinical terms – the players feel that they have taken part in something which reproduced the essential tactical conditions prevailing at the time and that nothing occurred to outrage anyone's sense of history. In this instance there is no question but that these conditions were fulfilled. Ordinarily, a considerable amount of reliance must be placed upon the goodwill and co-operation of the players in that they will not undertake any manoeuvre or tactic outside the spirit and practice of military operations of the period, but in Fontenoy the players were extremely well-versed in its military history and acted completely in accordance with this.

Linked to the feeling that a good representation of the battle had taken place was a natural and lively satisfaction that the wargame rules governing the operation were satisfactory, not simply because the historical result was repeated but that the game revealed no anomalies whatever in their composition. To be perfectly honest – if more than a little immodest – it would have been surprising had this been so, as the actual rules involved have been tested in every possible sort of conflict over a number of years and by many different wargamers, both in individual battles and in the context of a campaign. All this has shown that they are as nearly perfect as possible within ordinary limitations.

Of course, it was a trifle unfair on the latter-day 'Cumberland' that his terms of reference were confined to more or less the historical facts, and certainly, competent player that he was, had he found himself in such a position during a campaign, he would most certainly have avoided carrying out an attack on the Fontenoy position with the forces at his disposition. Certainly, it seems that he would have required a superiority of at least fifty per cent in infantry and artillery to have made the operation a success. This is not, of course, to say that 'Saxe' had simply to sit back and let events take their course. His action in supporting the Grassins in the

Wood of Barry was a wise one, and even more praise-worthy was his denuding the Redoubt d'Eu of its garrison and using it to enfilade the flank of the Allied column – an excellent piece of tactical thinking.

As mentioned already, the time element is an important one in such historical reconstructions as we have described. The 18 periods which covered the playing time and which amounted to something like 3 hours in the scale of ten minutes to a period seemed to give a reasonably accurate representation of fighting time, and could indeed represent an even longer period of combat. It is not really practicable to build into the wargame every possible cause of delay without rendering the whole affair tedious in the extreme. What I mean is this, to provide a simple example: an order emanates from the player (the 'general'), directed to a particular unit. Now the general might actually be with the unit concerned, and on the wargame table that unit will at once begin to carry out the order. What would happen in real life, however, would be that the general, despite his proximity, would sum up the situation, issue an order to an aide-de-camp, who would make his way to the colonel or commander of the regiment concerned, most prob-ably with a written order. The recipient reads and digests it, has a look at what his objective might be, then issues his own orders, probably to an adjutant or similar functionary. Thereafter follows the procedure of the regiment ordering its ranks, dressing, shouldering arms or whatever, whereupon the adjutant reports 'all ready' to the colonel, who then leads off his men. Thus, even in the speediest and most streamlined terms, the indi-vidual wargame periods have to be magnified many times to obtain a true perspective of time.

All this was very evident in our battle of Fontenoy, not only in the physical time but in the figurative time of the long advance of the infantry towards the French position. Considerable tension was evident on the part of the 'generals' and beads of perspiration became markedly apparent on upper lip and brow. All in all, as a wargame it was immensely enjoyable both to players and spectators, of whom there were not a few.

What then was the value of the exercise, apart from providing such interest and enjoyment? Simply, I feel, that it showed with some exactitude how a mid-18th Century army functioned and fought. It must not be thought that the value of the enterprise can be compressed into the actual number of hours during which the game was played, for the benefits derived are more far-reaching than that, when one considers the time devoted to valuable research into background material from both the British and French points of view. To draw conclusions from a study of the course of the historical battle and then by experiment to ascertain whether or not they were really valid is the nub of the entire situation. The result was not actually so important, but what was, in fact, was the resulting appreciation of the difficulties provided by a military situation, how they were exploited by one general and overlooked by another. It supplied much food for thought and a clearer picture of just what was involved in a major battle of more than two centuries ago.

13
Practicalities
of Wargaming
❖❖❖❖❖❖❖❖

That wargaming is a particularly gregarious pastime
cannot be in doubt, for obviously when someone has
realised the enormous pleasure to be obtained from
warfare in miniature, he will not be slow to seek out an
opponent with whom he can match his army and his
tactical skill. There do exist, of course, players who
prefer to wargame 'solo' – that is, with themselves controlling both sides. This does have certain advantages,
although one can imagine it giving rise to a fairly austere
and analytical sort of game, wherein fewer of the human
failings and errors which characterise the multi-player
battle will be found.

There are others, too, who are unfortunate enough to
live in a remote area or in one where enlightenment has
yet to penetrate, with a consequent sad dearth of enthusiasts and possible opponents! Happily however, thanks
to the phenomenal spread of interest in wargaming
which has marked the past five or six years, this category
of deprived persons is rapidly disappearing, although
certainly some unhappy ones still remain in sad isolation.

Nowadays, when it seems that virtually every town and city in the country has its military society or club, or at least an informal group of wargamers, there cannot be many unable to find themselves in the society of kindred spirits, with a minimum of effort.

Most such clubs will provide for a fairly catholic taste and will feature all kinds of wargames, from many periods, although occasionally one comes across some general preference or tendency. They will ordinarily cater for people of all ages, from the most junior in years to the most senior. They will be more or less organised, with a properly drawn-up constitution, elected officers and a committee, and will involve the payment of a small subscription to cover possible costs, such as the purchase of stationery, the hiring of a hall and so forth. They are a boon to the person who wishes to take part in activities of a general nature, or who likes, as many players do, to spread their wargaming between two or even more periods of history. Apart from such more formally constituted assemblies, there is the loose association of the like-minded, those whose wish it is to concentrate, possibly with some degree of seriousness, on some particular section of the art of war. This can be either on a competitive basis, with games played between two 'generals' possibly in the framework of a league or championship, or on certain historical battles, taking them for reconstitution and subsequent study and analysis – in much the same way as was done with Fontenoy, with all players taking part, save he who organised the particular operation and who is accordingly fully occupied in taking notes on its progress for resulting comparison with history. Where all are friends of like interests and tastes, it is certainly arguable that this is the most suitable milieu for congenial wargaming.

Leaving aside common interests and enthusiasms (which we take for granted), certain physical conditions are more or less mandatory for such an organisation, of which the first is that there should be a suitable venue for the wargames to be played. Within the group members it might be that there are several lucky enough to have at least a semi-permanent wargames set-up, or, better still, there may be one happy soul with an individual room which he can give up entirely to his hobby. Fortunate is he who is in this very agreeable position. Let us suppose, therefore, that one of the group or association has such a room and he has installed there a table for the express purpose of playing wargames. The size of this essential piece of furniture is of some importance, for obviously it must not be too small. Limitations of the available playing area and over-enthusiasm in regard to the number of figures deployed on it make for a very static kind of game where any sort of manoeuvre becomes more or less impossible. Everyone naturally has his favourite table shape, but I would suggest that a table varying between 7 ft. by 5 ft., and 9 ft. by 7 ft. would be found to be eminently suitable. Anything narrower than 5 ft. is really not desirable as, short of the approach moves being made along the length of the table, which horribly restricts the available combat front, the contending armies will start the operation much too close to each other.

Once a table and venue are available on a permanent basis, the tremendous advantages become immediately apparent. No battle – as can so frequently happen when the battlefield or playing area is not exclusive to the wargamers – has to be abandoned at a crucial moment when 'time is up'. In the fortunate and indeed ideal situation where a permanent wargame room exists, the action can be 'frozen' and left until the next occasion when the players are able to assemble and resume the action. It might be said that this possibly leads to a loss, or at least a lessening, of interest before play is again possible, but I can only quote from my own experience and say that this does not take place when the players are really keen. Indeed, just for the record, our Battle of Fontenoy occupied three separate sessions, and in the last interest was just as high as it had been during the first.

On the point of interest, too, there arises the question of what happens to the others when two players are occupied, for instance, in a challenge or competition game. It might be thought that with, say, eight or ten players forming the loose group we have envisaged, if many such games are played there will be some considerable lapse of time between those in which each player is directly involved as a combatant, and that participation in large multi-player battles may not be considered entirely sufficient for people of really competitive spirit. Again I must content that this need not be the case, for more thinking players can be interested for a considerable part of the time in watching – if not actually playing – other people play – or better still, in being involved in some way with the conduct of the game in progress.

It happens in this way.

First of all, I have yet to take part in or witness a wargame which has failed to produce some sort of situation not completely covered by the rules in use. The wargame rules have yet to be produced which are voluminous or comprehensive enough to give chapter and verse to decide every possible point which may arise. The best one can do is to lay down general principles which should allow a determination of any problem or doubt which may rear its querulous head. What I have in mind is the query concerned with the time factor. For instance, should a player announce his intention of charging some enemy unit with one of his own, possibly against an unprotected flank, does the recipient have the time or the opportunity to 'make a front' to meet this attack; will it be totally unexpected, or, just as bad, will he be caught in the act of changing formation? On occasion, no complete answer to such questions will be readily apparent within the arbitrary 'periods' into which the game is customarily divided and it is in such circumstances that a disinterested party is able to adjudicate and make a decision on what would be the most probable course of events. This can be frequently done by working in 'quarter periods', a very useful method of resolving such time difficulties. Then there are the times when our arbiter has to concern himself with the proper carrying out of orders which have been given to units. In most games – I venture to say in all serious wargames – some sort of written orders or at least declarations of intent have to be committed to paper, for groups of regiments or for individual ones. Human nature being what it is, the 'umpire' must on occasion ensure that the spirit of such orders is not overly strained by the player's making a regiment behave otherwise than in accordance with the instructions already given to it.

So, in accordance with these *obiter dicta,* it is obvious that one of the non-fighting members of the group should be elected to the position of 'umpire'. Naturally enough, he would tend to be one of the most experienced of those present. In a game when two players begin with an evenly balanced pair of armies he will check that their forces are of equivalent power, with reference to the particular points scheme which is operative – and he will superintend any manoeuvres which might be carried out on maps before action is transferred to the actual wargames table.

In connection with this, if I may digress a little, it should be pointed out that such map 'activity' is a very useful manner of cutting down the time occupied in the 'approach' moves – that is, those resulting when armies are laid down on opposing base lines of the table and have to plod across its width before coming into contact. If 'gridded' maps are prepared of the wargame terrain, the initial moves can be made thereon, rather than by moving masses of figures on the table itself. Not only is this a potent time-saver, but when the system involves each player informing the other only of the grid references of his moves (the map can be divided for convenience into squares of 1 in. equalling 1 ft. on the table) it ensures that at least a modicum of the fog of war surrounds the players. Although each is appraised of the other's presence in a particular grid square, he has initially no idea of what might be there – it could be a couple of infantry battalions or a mere scouting party of a handful of cavalry. In passing, it can be pointed out that what this represents is information gleaned from interrogation of the local populace, brief sightings of the reflection of light on bayonet or lance point, a suspicious cloud of dust and so on.

When the map moves have brought portions of the contending forces to a point within an agreed limit of proximity then map movement is suspended and the wargame troops are placed in their correct positions on the table. Important exceptions would be those who, during the map moving, had entered woods, wherein they would be invisible to an enemy, or who are out of sight behind hills. Such eventualities, of course, also come within the aegis of the umpire whose further duty it would be to ensure the correct placing of troops and to check as to whether any concealed units are actually outside any possible enemy line of vision.

From the foregoing we can see that an umpire is more than fully occupied with his multifarious duties, so we have to allocate some of the tasks remaining to others who may be present. For one such, this is certainly an easy matter. Many of the sets of rules now in general use have systems of casualties based, not upon actual wargame figures, but upon the proportional number of fighting men they represent, this in many cases being in the nature of 1 wargame figure to 20 actual men. At the same time the corresponding casualty charts are scaled with the latter in mind, so that as a result of enemy action, we can have such losses as 13, 21 or 35, to give but three examples. This means, following the 1 equals 20 concept, that when figure casualties are removed from the table, generally at the end of the period for which the assessment is being made, then some part, if we take the second and third of our examples, will have to be 'carried over', while in the first, the 13 stated does not represent a complete figure, so none will be removed.

Thus a small amount of 'book-keeping' becomes

necessary, this being carried out on a simple form divided firstly into *periods* (these being numbered 1, 2, 3 and so on as the game proceeds) and being further sub-divided into three columns – and this is only a suggestion – which we can call *casualties, figures taken off* and *carried forward*. This is self-explanatory, but in brief, as casualties occur in a unit – from a variety of causes: artillery fire, musketry, etc – they are noted in column one, and at the end of the period the appropriate figures are removed, any remainder being noted in the third column to be added to whatever is suffered during the following period. Without a 'scorer' the players will have to charge themselves with this chore, which is distracting and prevents the game flowing as smoothly as it might otherwise do.

There are other tasks which might be found proper – other than that of 'assistant umpire', of whom there is often a plethora, all ready, willing and generous in their giving of gratuitous advice! These can well be occupied in measuring ranges, movement distances concerned in morale assessments – such as those involved when it becomes necessary to determine how much support a unit has within a prescribed distance – and quite certainly there are other tasks which can be given to spectators. In my own circle these are happily ready and eager to assume such minor responsibilities.

The above are but a few ideas which stem from a fairly long wargaming experience. They are not set down as immutable dogma but merely to provide some sort of guide-line to the newcomer to the hobby, and possibly even to the more experienced wargamer.

14
Wargame Campaigning
in the 18th Century
◇◆◇◆◇◆◇◆◇◆◇◆◇

As the wargamer progresses in experience and expertise
– and this is the customary course of events – it is
almost inevitable that at some time he will feel the
desire to have some sort of background to what he is
doing. He will come to the conclusion that, however
satisfying the individual battles in which he has participated, be they speculative tactical problems or
carefully researched examinations and refights of actual
historical engagements – such as we have attempted to
consider in this book – there should be a rather more
comprehensive *raison d'être* for his operations.

In spite of the good will of the players, there will
almost certainly be a tendency at some time or other for
one of them to take some action or to execute some
tactical manoeuvre which would be incorrect or im-
proper were it to happen within a general strategic
framework. In most ordinary wargames the onus is on
each player to defeat or destroy his enemy there and then,
and such circumstances completely ignore the numerous
engagements throughout history where the context was

vastly different, and where, for instance, a small force was fighting a delaying action in an endeavour to gain time for reinforcements to arrive, or conversely, to hold up an enemy army to allow one's own main body to escape. It is also a matter of experience that quite frequently small actions – skirmishes between parties of scouting cavalry or ambushes laid by companies of light infantry for example – are often more exciting and realistic than many major battles. What all this is leading up to is the proposition that the most enjoyable and successful wargaming is that involved in the conduct of campaign rather than in the fighting of individual battles more or less *in vacuo*.

Now, it goes without saying that a considerable amount of good will is necessary for participation in this sort of 'advanced wargaming' (I am not too sure that I care much for this description but can think of no other at the moment). Preparations are necessary, not a little book-keeping is required and, in default of an umpire or co-ordinator, one must on every occasion be scrupulously fair in carrying out troop movements and other operations which will be outside the immediate ken of one's opponent. There is, however, as in most wargaming activities, an easy way out, should it be so desired, and the one which comes most readily to the mind is the system whereby one fights a series of battles, with pre-determined armies, and the result of each will have an influence on the location and meaning of the next, as well as on the numerical ratios of the troops involved on the opposing sides. This can work out pretty success-fully, and may well be worth attempting as a beginning to campaigning.

One can take, for instance, an area which was the scene of some actual campaign and stage one's battles thereon. I recall fighting such a campaign in an American Civil War context, using a large sheet of paper 'gridded' into squares (actually they were rectangles in this particular case), each equalling the area – to an agreed scale, naturally – of the wargame table in use at the time. The

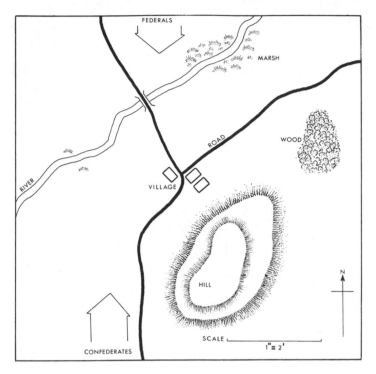

Map 8. Setting up a campaign – the initial battle. Scale 1″ = 2′ on wargame's table

initial battle was set up, fought to a conclusion and the terrain which had figured on the wargames table transferred to one of the squares on the previously prepared sheet, this first one, to ensure some sort of equality, being more or less near the centre of the complete map. Upon the result of this first battle was more or less decided the theme and position of that which followed. I say 'more or less' because the numerous conflicts making up the series were derived from various sources, some being purely imaginary in forces, topography and so on, while others were specific tactical problems – such as one wherein one player had to ensure the passage of a convoy from one side of the wargames table to the other, while his opponent's aim was to prevent this – or at least

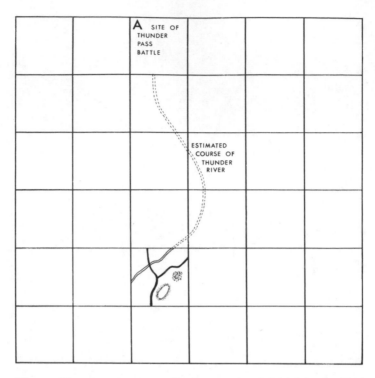

Map 9. The campaign map, showing terrain of initial battle. Each square equals the size of the wargame's table

to hold up the convoy's movement. Yet others were based upon actual engagements which took place in the Civil War itself. A considerable amount of imagination, not to say speculation, had to go into the building up of the theoretical background as well as the creation of the terrain, and possibly an example might be sufficient to suggest just how the whole enterprise was accomplished.

First then, let us suppose that Map 8 was of the first battle actually fought, and in it the Confederates scored a decisive victory, and coming from the south, drove the enemy, the Federal force, completely off the wargames table. With this battle therefore dealt with, its terrain was transferred – much reduced in scale of course – to one of the central squares of Map 9 as we can see. This second map is, as it were, the blank cheque for the campaign, and upon its virgin area would gradually be built up the entire area over which the 'campaign' was being fought. With this done, then, the next battle was decided upon and it was fought, in fact, as a Federal defence of a fairly rugged valley – in point of fact it was called Thunder Pass, a most evocative title, one of many which came very readily to the imagination. As might have been expected, the Confederate attack on the strongly defended Federal position in Thunder Pass was flung back with some considerable loss, and the 'Rebs' retired to re-group.

Meantime, the 'Thunder Pass' area had to be transferred to the main map, the question being just where? Well, the river running diagonally across Map 8 will have been noticed, I do not doubt, and, as it happened, a river also ran through Thunder Pass. It seemed logical, therefore, to link up the two, and so – to allow for a fairly gentle curving of the stream, the site of the Thunder Pass battle was inserted in the overall map three clear squares north of the first encounter, this being indicated on Map 9 as 'A'. This also allowed for the fact that the Federal defeat in the first fight had been so severe as to ensure that the remnants of the force engaged would have certainly retreated – the word is used with extreme looseness – at least two or three table widths before a halt was made.

So Thunder Pass took its place on Map 9, and at the same time the full course of the newly entitled Thunder River was drawn in across the adjacent squares, as shown by the dotted lines. Thus we have the beginnings of a general map of a territory into which all sorts of combats and battles could be fitted. In actual fact it was found to be quite remarkable just how speedily the numerous squares were filled up, many by the transfer of terrain used in an actual wargame from the table, or in some cases by creating map details in, say, a single square separating two whose details had already been inserted.

It was all great fun, and, for a not-too-complicated

sort of campaign it was highly satisfactory, particularly as we – the participants – allowed ourselves fairly free play in the nomenclature of the topographical features we invented. I have already mentioned Thunder Pass and Thunder River – the latter, as it transpired, due to play a major role in the campaign as a whole, many battles being fought up and down its length. 'Ghost Valley' there' was, and also 'The Defence of Vulture Ridge', and the very last battle of the campaign resulted in the Confederates – sad to say, as the writer was in command – being driven by overwhelming Federal forces into a singularly unpleasant area known appropriately as 'Alligator Swamp'! All in all, the enterprise was most enjoyable and highly instructive in that it prepared the ground for future and rather more involved campaigning.

Of course, all the foregoing has been but a species of preamble to our main theme, which concerns wargame campaigning in a period much closer to, and indeed contemporary with the battle which has been the subject of the present study. This, of course, comprises the middle years of the 18th Century – and in my opinion there is no era in military history more suitable for this particular wargame purpose. It has already been pointed out in the introduction to the study of warfare in what we can call 'our period' that the middle decades of the 18th Century provide a time of complete professionalism in both the theory and the practice of war. It is consequently one in which we need have no truck with popular movements, ideologies, the influence of public opinion and the like. Hence, in our campaigning we need have no concern with anything other than strictly military manoeuvres and logistics, in contrast to those who would campaign for instance in the Spain of Napoleonic times, when guerilla activities played such an important part in military operations, and where certainly one of the contending forces had to 'live off the country', with resultant complications of dispersal and foraging – and where an actively inimical populace completely inhibited any attempt to shroud one's movements in secrecy.

With all these built-in advantages in mind, then, one can proceed with some practical ideas for setting up and conducting a campaign located sometime between the years 1740 to 1760. I have in fact done this with complete success and with a high degree of realism on several occasions, some of the campaigns lasting several months, both in real and in wargame time. Naturally no suggestion is necessarily made that campaigns need be so prolonged – this, like so many facets of the wargame, is largely a matter of personal preference. As players become more and more involved in the operations they are conducting, and as they see their well laid plans come to successful fruition or, conversely, collapse in total disarray, so they will often find themselves planning for events well ahead in time, and soon they will find themselves committed willy-nilly to an extent possibly far beyond their original intention.

Having thus mentally prepared ourselves for what is to come, the first – obvious – thing to be done is to make a decision about the map of the territory where the fighting is to take place. Assuming that we have already decided that the rather elementary system explained earlier, wherein *ad hoc* battles are fought and subsequently integrated into a prepared 'grid', is not going to be acceptable, something a little more sophisticated and realistic will be required. Initially, then, we have to make the important choice as to whether the map is to be a real one of an actual area of some suitable country, or whether it will be something completely imaginary, but nevertheless containing all the natural topographical features to be found, for instance, in a present-day Ordnance Survey Map. The advantage of the first is that it is certainly 'real' country, with towns, villages, roads and so on, but the trouble is that almost certainly too many of these features will be found to be incompatible with a time when urban development was far less than it is today. Upon the natural features of a modern map will also be superimposed spreading tentacles of railways, electric grid systems, motorways and so on, none of which existed in our mid-18th Century period.

One can search, of course, for sections of modern maps where the territory is pretty wild, and which has little in the way of built-up area with its inevitable concomitants of transport and communication, but it will generally be found that this will result in regions so mountainous or in other ways inaccessible, as to be totally unsuitable. We may as well accept the obvious then, which is that a prepared, imaginary map should be used. This solution, in my own experience, is far more suitable for the purpose we have in mind, and any trouble in its construction is far outweighed by the practical benefits accruing.

When contemplating the drawing of one's own map, it is immediately apparent that the essential operation of 'gridding' must be carried out. This gridding has the enormous advantage of directly relating the map to the size of the wargame table in use, much as, in the simple system already described, the table area 'slotted' into one of the blank squares on the map. This provides advantages which will become clear as we proceed. Another benefit is, of course, that the players can incorporate exactly the sort of terrain they desire in the area being covered. I hasten to add, of course, that the terrain *can* be based upon an actual area, leaving out such anachronistic details as railways and so on, but, all things being considered, I have found it easier and more suitable to create a completely mythical stretch of country. This can then be as characterful or as featureless as the players wish, or as suitable as possible for the type of campaign to be fought upon it.

As an extreme example of what I mean, it could be that the players wish to reconstitute some phase of the middle 18th Century French and Indian Wars in America, this involving a practically uninterrupted area of dense forest, interspersed with rivers, lakes and streams. Alternatively, should the wish be – as ours is – to stage a campaign in the Low Countries of Europe, then the terrain features can be adjusted accordingly.

As it is then our purpose to integrate our activities into the European scene, with the normal topographical features, plus towns, cities and road systems, we must first provide ourselves with a stout sheet of paper, large enough to cover the necessary area. This we 'grid' into areas, each of which represents the size of the table we are going to use for the actual fighting. For simplicity – always a good thing – we postulate that the table measures 8 ft. by 8 ft., and the grid squares will be representative of this. Again, in an attempt to reduce our labours we can use a commercially produced sheet of graph paper, gridded in 1 in. squares, and if one can ignore the secondary grid lines – they *never* coincide with any sort of table scale – we can save time by using such a paper. In either case then, with the sheet of paper divided into 1 in. squares, before us, we start to lay out our imaginary terrain. Rather than give a blow-by-blow account of this a better idea is to illustrate a small section of such a wargame map and point out its various features as we progress. So, the reader's attention is directed to Map 10, which, it goes without saying, is imaginary, and which – and this is the important thing – contains all the various terrain features, hills, roads and so on, together with towns and villages, which, as we shall see, have a very important function.

Possibly the first detail to be noted is that there are no 'blanks' (for want of a better word), every square containing some sort of feature. Each also has either a major or a minor road running through it. It has already been pointed out that armies of this period did not take kingly to wandering about across country during a campaign, their rate of movement being, in truth, slow enough without having to step out across farming land, ploughed fields and so on. Experience shows that it is better to ensure, by the presence of a road, that troops can move into or through each and every square on the

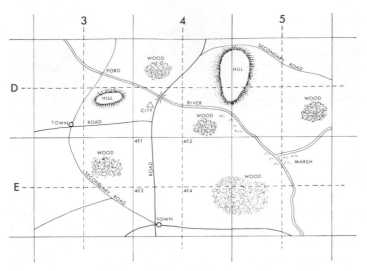

Map 10. Section of wargame map

map. There is one notable exception to this rule, but of that more anon. In drawing up the map, the player will naturally ensure that the different forms of terrain are properly identified, and a little time spent with water-colour is of the greatest possible advantage, and the effect is itself not unaesthetic when we contemplate hills shaded in brown of various depths to represent different heights, woods in green and rivers and lakes naturally in blue. I repeat that it is a matter of inclination just how much trouble is spent on the map but, as it will, hope-fully, be used for quite a time, why not take that little extra trouble?

One other point which must be mentioned, although its purpose will be dealt with more fully in its proper place, is the double system of 'gridding'. It will be seen that the continuous lines enclose squares each sub-divided into four smaller squares – it is these smaller ones which represent the table areas, incidentally – and that both sizes of square can readily be identified. Right in the centre of our specimen map we have the major square '4E' whose component sub-squares are lettered

4E1 and 4E2, these being the upper pair, while the lower ones are 4E3 and 4E4. This type of identification applies to the entire map, and by this means reference can be made to any area which has to be reproduced on a wargames table when action thereon becomes inevitable. The purpose of the double system of square identification may not be at once apparent, but all will – in due course – be revealed.

Now that we have familiarised ourselves with the appearance of at least a small portion of the proposed campaigning map, the first step – and it is a vital one, indeed – is to establish a relationship between troop movements on the map and those taking place on the table. Now, in our general remarks on the practice of the wargame (Chapter Nine) we laid down a number of simple laws, among which was the precept that the ordinary marching rate for infantry is 60 yards per minute which, in terms of our table scale, was represented by a distance of 6 in. This really represents a 'mean', the average rate of progress which could be maintained for some considerable time, making allowance for occasional 'doubling', for the rest periods when the troops fall out for a 'breather', and so on. As a speed, therefore, it is perfectly suited for use in campaigning terms as a route march rate.

It is upon this 6 in. per move concept that we base our map moves. Obviously, for convenience, a 'map move' or 'period' will have to consist of a number of table 'periods' and we calculate this quite simply. At 6 in. per move, our infantry will cross from one side of our 8 ft. table to the other in 16 periods, so it is convenient – experience tells us so – to divide this 16 by four and to state that four 'table' periods equal one 'day' in our campaign time. Now, I shall not dwell upon the obvious anomaly of having 16 times a single minute making up a whole campaigning day – say of eight hours action time – but the system works very well and indeed realistically. We must not forget the built-in natural delays which would be impracticable to include as part of the imponderable of the wargame – when there is a breakdown in the transmission of orders, messengers lose their way, troops arrive at bridges which are 'down' or at fords where rivers are unexpectedly in flood – all these things together with the inevitable slowing down as orders move along the chain of command. All these factors have to be taken for granted, and we achieve this, partly at least, by allowing for them in the slower campaign move. We do so for all arms, of course – cavalry, artillery and so forth – and for the first of these we have a longer map move in the same way and in the same proportion as we did for cavalry upon the actual table. Now it is a fact not often completely appreciated that mounted troops over long journeys do not necessarily move many times more rapidly than their dismounted counterparts, despite what one's preconceived ideas – usually stemming from the visual media – might suggest. Without going into a great deal of chapter and verse, let me state quite briefly that a route move for cavalry – and this includes periods of 'walk', shorter periods of 'trot', intervals during which riders dismount and lead their mounts, and actual periods of 'halt' when girths are slackened and so on – would be approximately only twice as fast as that of infantry.

With this fact in mind, we can readily lay down the map moves for both cavalry and infantry, and without more ado we say that on our map – with one of the smaller squares representing a table area – infantry may move $\frac{1}{4}$ in. and cavalry $\frac{1}{2}$ in. This is all very fine, but my personal experience is that such moves are really too short and tend to create errors when the players are conducting their moves on the map. My suggestion therefore is that the periods per day be shortened from four to two, this having the effect of doubling the map moves, thus making that for cavalry 1 in. and for infantry $\frac{1}{2}$ in. Again, this suggestion comes from a not inconsiderable experience in dealing with such campaigns as we are describing. I think we can now leave the matter of map moves without further expanding upon the subject, although much could be said about transport and artillery movement. As far as the latter is concerned, it may be appropriate to remind the reader that we are here talking about foot artillery – with the gunners trudging along beside their cannon – and its speed would therefore be the same as for infantry. There is also the question as to whether wheeled vehicles, including guns of course, should be limited to roads and not allowed – on the map at least – to move across country in any circumstances. This is a decision to be made by the individual wargamer in the light of his experience and preferences.

Hastening on, then, let us imagine our players each provided with a map of the relevant country, and with details of his own army, its strength, composition and so on. He decides upon the disposition of his troops, considers his objectives and makes his plans accordingly. In the ideal situation there should really be a third individual (a sort of umpire or controller) to whom each player would – naturally in secret – communicate movement of troops and similar intelligence. This third party would in turn give the other player such information as the latter would be deemed properly to have ascertained. However, as it is not possible to have the services of such a third party at all times, then the system will have to provide for the players themselves being responsible for the passing of information to each other. Fortunately this is a problem really very easily resolved. Ordinarily, in wargaming, I feel it desirable for moves to be made simultaneously, but the exception to this rule is the present case where, for various reasons, it will be found better for the players to make their moves alternately. Principally, it obviates any chance of accidental 'by passing' if map moves are declared by each player in turn, and it is perfectly easy, of course, when any transposition has to be made from map to fighting area, to ensure that the player who has made his 'declaration of moves' after the other will have the opportunity of adjusting such moves so that the table action, should it

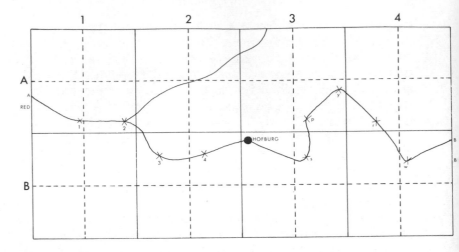

Map 11. Action demonstrated on section of campaign map. For clarity only roads are shown

materialise, becomes very properly simultaneous.

For an example of how two wargamers go about the business, your attention is drawn to Map 11, which is a version of a small area of the overall campaign map. Let us imagine that Player *Red* is moving on to the map from the left and that his opponent, whom we shall not surprisingly denominate *Blue*, is approaching from the right. For the purposes of the demonstration, each has a small force of cavalry, and the object of the exercise, from both points of view, is to carry out a reconnaissance of the village of Hofburg – to be seen in the centre of the map – where enemy activity has been reported. For no good reason let us say that *Red* moves first and he accordingly notes that his cavalry – having moved 1 in. from the point of arrival at 'A' has reached point '1'. Having done this, he now makes his declaration to the opposing player by simply pronouncing the formula '1.A', thereby informing him that somewhere in this general area there are some *Red* troops, but of their number and nature no information is naturally forthcoming. Still 'off the map' to the right *Blue* now has some indication of enemy activity, such as might be derived from the questioning of local peasantry, from distant views of clouds of dust, or, depending upon the weather, the glint of sunshine on weapons or equipment. Being an active commander, *Blue* loses no time in taking steps to find out what this activity in '1A' may be. He accordingly launches his own reconnaissance party of cavalry on to the map at 'B' and, with them also moving at the 1 in. per period speed, they arrive at 'w', and it is then *Blue's* turn to 'declare' this being, of course, '4B'. This declaration gives to *Red* the same sort of general information he himself has already received. Both reconnaissances are now well and truly under way and we shall rapidly see what transpires.

Back to *Red* now for the next period, and naturally he pushes forward the prescribed inch and gives his delaration as '1A'. *Blue* in turn similarly speaks out, thus – '4A'. Two further periods result in two declarations from *Red* of '2B' and also the additional mention of '2A' (through which he passed during the third period), this, incidentally, serving to confuse the issue as far as *Blue* is concerned, the possibility being at once apparent that *Red* has either moved south or is still in '2A', or indeed that there might be two separate forces on the move. *Blue's* declarations were straightforward for the two periods, his 1 in. moves taking him to points 'y' and 'p' respectively. The next move and its consequent declaration are somewhat crucial, as discovery and confrontation are very important. *Red* naturally again pushes forward, his 1 in. move taking his men into HOFBURG itself, where, he finds only the populace going about its lawful occasions, and no sign of the enemy. *Blue* likewise moves ahead, his 1 in. taking his party to point 's', located in the second sub-square of '3B'.

Here the procedure alters somewhat, indeed becoming more particular for, as *Red* has already stated that he is in '3B', *Blue* must not only give the major but the minor square as well, to wit, 3B2. The absence of reaction at once throws some light on the situation, as *Blue* must now be aware that, coming from the west along the road, *Red* must of necessity be in 3B1. When it comes to *Red's* turn, he may elect to remain ensconced in HOFBURG, but as for *Blue*, if he advances, he must particularise, as the sub-square is already occupied, and he does so – '3B1'. The onus is now upon *Blue*, who, in the event, thereupon advances and himself declares his presence in '3B1'.

So the confrontation has occurred and the players must now decide upon the consequences. In the present instance, each might, to save the time occupied in transferring the terrain of 3B1 to the wargames table, simply announce to the other the fact that he had a cavalry patrol in the area consisting, possibly, of half a dozen men, maybe an officer, trumpeter and a few troopers. Naturally, in default of a physical 'set-down', the players would be furnished with details of the uniform of the enemy troops, for identification purposes. This 'intelligence' would obviously be the sort of thing a scouting party would wish to transmit to headquarters to assist in the location of enemy units. It goes without saying that either player, should he so wish, can insist on a 'set-down'. One might have, in fact, not just a patrol of half-a-dozen men but possibly a full squadron, and might accordingly think it a good idea to drive off the enemy *sans façon*. Even this, of course, may be conducted upon paper, although, for instance, should the small patrol have a follow-up force in close attendance, maybe in the adjacent square, he may elect to fight to allow time for reinforcements to come up to his assistance. If both wargamers are similarly disposed, with substantial cavalry following up, then we have all the makings of a goodly cavalry encounter. It should be pointed out before we proceed further that in the case of support troops in adjacent squares, their time of arrival on the actual table can readily be calculated on the map/table move ratio to ensure their appearance at the proper time.

What has just been described is naturally the most

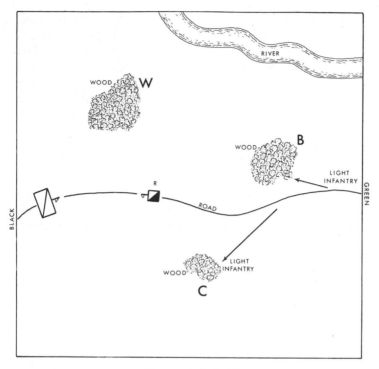

Map 12. 'Ambush'

simple example which can come to mind, but its permutations and variations are almost endless, and another
simple example may be of some interest.

It will be recalled that we have suggested as a general
rule that, on the map, all troops must move on roads, but
there must be exceptions to this, of course, one of these
being the situation where a force has to take up a specific
position. Let us illustrate this once more by precept,
which will in addition demonstrate, it is hoped, how the
map game lends itself to the exploitation of surprise and
the 'fog of war'. This we can do by studing Map 12
which is, in effect, a single sub-square from the general
campaign map, not forgetting that, should a set-down
arise, it will be reproduced on the wargame's table
exactly as shown. Let us imagine that Force 'A' has

arrived there some time previously, possibly three or four map periods before, and that it consists of a cavalry troop and a couple of companies of light infantry. The cavalry troop is positioned by the player – we shall designate him *Green*, just for a change – as shown, having moved along the road from the point of entry on the right. At the same time the two infantry companies are moved *off* the road, one veering north and the other south, and when the cavalry has taken up its position, the light infantrymen have disappeared into the two small woods, where they are totally concealed. On succeeding period 'declarations' Green affirms his presence in the large square of which our map is a part, until finally his enemy – *Black*, naturally – locates him, and, on the map, moves into the sub-square from the west. *Green*, for his part, admits to being present there, but demands a set-down, and when this has been done, we have *Black's* squadron – for so it turned out to be – facing *Green's* cavalry troop, much smaller of course. It will be patently obvious that *Green's* jäger – it seems that they were vaguely Germanic – are absolutely invisible. *Green* would at this stage inform the umpire – in conditions of complete secrecy, of course – of their presence. Should there be no such functionary, *Green* would note the facts of position and strength concerning the light infantry on a piece of paper which ideally would be sealed and placed in a position ready for production when the time is ripe. Seeing *Green's* small force, *Black* will probably wish to drive it off to the east, and advances towards it, although, being not without experience, he will suspect the motives of his enemy and look with some concern upon the nearby woods. As it happens, *Green* falls back with some deliberation, passing wood 'W', while his enemy follows up pretty gingerly, and finding nothing emerging with malice aforethought from that particular wood, pushes on with a little more confidence until, lured into a position between 'B' and 'C' woods, the light infantry concealed there suddenly appear, lining the edges of the trees and pouring a destructive fire of muskets into *Black's* cavalrymen. The latter – or the survivors possibly – will certainly decide to call it a day, rushing off in great disarray, leaving a not inconsiderable number of casualties on the stricken field. The point need hardly be made that this is a very elementary sort of proceeding and no commander worthy of his salt would fall into what was really a very obvious trap, but it is emphasised that this is merely the essence of what can happen in the process of employing surprise in map and table moves. Much more elaborate stratagems can be used with success, and can involve artillery as well as cavalry and infantry.

Apart from organising such small scale ambuscades as we have described, entire armies may in this way be deployed in an individual sub-square to await the advent of an expected attack, for naturally generals would wish to take advantage of a position favourable to themselves. By this token, then, we can visualise in the case of the major battle which has been the subject of this study that the player whose role was that of Marshal Saxe would have entered the sub-square covering the Anthoing–Fontenoy–Wood of Barry area and disposed his forces in the manner in which we have shown, while awaiting the arrival of 'Cumberland'. It is of course obvious that in such a case, with the battle being an integral part of a campaign and with the choice open to 'Cumberland' as to whether to press home the attack or not, he might well, had he been in complete possession of his faculties, have opted to retire to seek a more advantageous battle another day. As I have tried to point out, this is the true *raison d'être* of wargaming – it should dispense utterly with any sort of 'let's have a go' philosophy, or at least it should in well-regulated wargaming circles!

In discussing the possibilities involved in laying on a species of ambush, mention was made of how the surprised side retreated, leaving its casualties upon the field or, in other words, having a number of its miniature figures removed as being *hors de combat*. In an individual battle the degree of incapacity of these casualties is irrelevant, for once they have fallen they are out of action for the entire wargame. This, however, is not so when a campaign is in progress, wherein wounded may possibly be collected by their fellows, subjected to the rudimentary medical skills of the time and may possibly, with some luck, be restored at a future date to active service. This is not really the place to discuss at any length the medical science of the time – it was from all accounts more than a little primitive – but it is important to establish a proportion relating to those having received a permanent quietus and those who were wounded, with reference especially to those severely wounded and those whose hurts were only of a slight or superficial nature. Simplicity, as always, being our watchword, we shall confine ourselves to enumerating an elementary ratio for wargame use, by which we stipulate that, of the figures removed from the table in any sort of engagement, one fifth are 'dead', one fifth are very lightly wounded and may return to duty the day following their wounding, one fifth will be fit in five days, another fifth in ten and the remaining fifth in fifteen days. Now these proportions and times of recovery are completely arbitrary and serve only as a convenient yardstick which has been found to work well in practice.

Having accepted these figures, we have to proceed to the curative process and where it will take place. At once we face the problem of how our casualties are to be removed from the field of battle, and it is a self-evident fact that in the case of the force which was ambushed and whose survivors fled in some haste, that there is no one to do so, and that the wounded left behind must necessarily be considered to be prisoners of war. It is fair to say that, if wounded are to be manhandled from the field, the more seriously wounded will need much more in the way of assistance than the 'walking wounded', for example. I think it fair to assume that the latter would require no actual help – or at least it might be reasonable to establish this as a basis from which to work – while the very seriously wounded would have to have the assistance of two, possibly even three, of their unwounded comrades, these numbers being for the individual wargamer to choose.

Once the wounded have been removed from the actual scene of the fighting, this by their fellows of course, other circumstances will become operative and we shall have to make one or two assumptions as to their future disposal. Should the battle in question have taken place in one's own national territory, then it is reasonable to suppose that the services of the local populace would be called upon to provide farm wagons and other suitable vehicles to transport the sufferers to wherever – for want of a better word – a hospital has been set up. This means that no actual troops would have to be diverted for this humanitarian purpose. On the other hand, should one's operations have taken one's army into enemy territory, it would be highly unlikely that the locals would provide any assistance and thus when an army is fighting in foreign territory it has to provide its own transport for wounded. The provision of this in anticipation of such a circumstance is but one element in the problem of logistics which can be as complex or as simple as the participants desire. In any case, transport, customarily in the shape of waggons, will have to be provided – so many to each regiment or brigade – for the conveyance of ammunition and supplies, and certainly in the days when field entrenchments were readily erected – as indeed we saw was the case at Fontenoy – each army would be obliged to have its quota of engineer waggons, to carry the picks, spades and other such paraphernalia.

At this point, it might be as well to point out that it is perfectly easy to calculate, for wargame purposes, the time it takes a given number of men to construct such-and-such a length of fortification or breastwork. These will be found extremely useful when, for instance, a small force has to make some sort of defence against a stronger attacker. Further, at the time with which we are concerned, such field works were dug by the ordinary line infantry under the direction of the engineers, who were in fact a species of officer corps in most armies. Thus, when building up a wargame army with a view to engaging in the sort of campaign we are considering, the quota of engineers with the correct number of waggons for the size of the particular force would have to be considered with some care. This is rather in contrast to the provision of medical staff, whose existence we can imagine, particularly, as being non-combatant personnel, they have no positive role to play, as do the engineers. That is not to say, of course, that the player should not have, if he wishes, his miniature figures representing *chirurgien* and assistants.

The reference to the establishment of the middle 18th Century variation of what, with some looseness, we might call 'hospitals' leads us on to consider their location. The most likely would be in a city or a town, hopefully at some distance from possible enemy activity. This possibility leads us on to think of the occupation of one's territory by an enemy force and what effect this can have on operations. The first point to be considered is that the normal wear and tear of campaigning – skirmishes, battles and so on – will reduce the available forces, either through actual casualties or the losing of prisoners to enemy hands. Ordinarily, one could and should expect replacements or recruits to flow in during the campaign to replenish such gaps, and for practical wargame campaign purposes, this can be organised quite simply, it being done in the following manner. At some pre-determined time, let us say for convenience each twentieth campaign day, a certain number of 'recruits' are activated at some convenient place in one's country, this usually being either the army headquarters or the capital city. This can be a stipulated and a standard number, common to both sides, but what has been found to be much better is a variable number of such replacements. This presupposes the existence of a specific 'points' value for every sort of soldier, and every vehicle and gun existing in the armies. For instance, an ordinary light infantryman might be valued at 1 point, a trained light infantryman at 2, and a heavy cavalryman at 5, a gun at 25 and so on. It can be enacted, then, that on the specified day, the twentieth as we suggested, 300 points worth – this is just a suggestion – of troops or material (depending upon the choice of the player), can be activated at capital or headquarters as appropriate. This, however, can be much improved upon as follows:

Instead of an arbitrary number, common to both armies, it is recommended that a note is made of the total losses in points value that each side has suffered during the twenty days of the period, and each player will receive replacements of the *lower* of the two totals. For example, should *Blue* army have suffered 320 points worth of losses during the time, and *Green* 400 points, then *both* sides receive 320 points of replacements, this leaving *Green*, sadly, 80 points short. What this means is that there is a considerable advantage accruing to the player whose armies have inflicted greater losses upon the enemy than have been received. There is, however, one important proviso, and it concerns the actual sources whence come these replacements. We are at once returned to the matter of cities and towns. The recruits whose mustering is eagerly expected will naturally come from every section of one's territory, but if any part of it is occupied by the enemy then it can hardly be expected to carry out its recruit commitments. An occupying force would tend to take a dim view of bodies of 'rookies' being spirited away to take service with an enemy! This must also apply therefore to a wargame campaign, but it would necessitate a considerable amount of book-keeping to maintain a record of areas occupied and for how long, so we use a simpler but none the less as efficient and correct a system, which can be briefly described. It depends, in fact, on occupied built-up areas, towns, cities and villages, if it is deemed proper to include the latter.

With this in mind we examine yet another section of

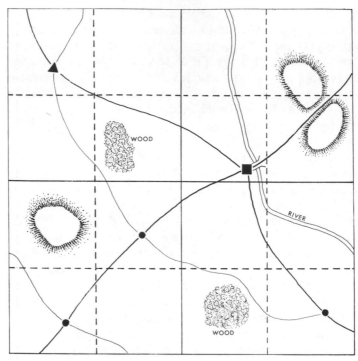

Map 13. Cities and towns

our campaign map, this being Map 13. This we can see to be a fairly well populated area – and it is in fact, for the purposes of the demonstration, that immediately surrounding a capital city. Obviously the various symbols represent different sizes of urban developments, and the square is the country's capital (there will be only one such on the whole map, naturally), the triangles are 'cities' and the 'circles' mere towns. These categories are arbitrary and are simple through necessity only. To have such a system will depend upon the players having drawn up their own map and having allocated a definite proportion of towns and cities commensurate with the production of recruits and replacements for the armies in accordance with the system we have described. A city will produce more recruits than will a town, the 'capital' producing even more. So, when compiling our map, we distribute an appropriate number of each category with this in mind. As a rough standard, may it be suggested that a 'capital' is responsible for 10% of recruits, a city for 5% and a 'town' for a lowly 2%. Just as an example let us postulate that we have our single capital city – 10%, 19 cities at 5% making up 50% and 20 towns at 2% making 40%, the total being the complete hundred. With these positioned on the map the rest is easy, this being the calculation of how much and in what manner the occupation of these areas affects the production of replacements.

Certainly, it will have to be enacted that a mere raid or similar incursion will be insufficient to stop the flow of recruits, and it must be decided what length of enemy occupation will suffice to disrupt the processes of induction and mustering. Here I have to say that I am now falling back on experience to suggest that – bearing in mind the fact that we are working on replacement periods of twenty days – an occupation for at least eight clear days out of the twenty will be enough to prevent the levying of recruits, and will reduce the national 'intake' by the appropriate percentage, whether it be the 2% of a 'town' or the 5% of a 'city' – Heaven forfend that it should be the 10% of one's capital!

Now, it may be recalled that the replacements were calculated – on each twentieth day – on the total points value of losses suffered by the side with the lesser loss total. An example may clarify the situation. Let us say that on this particular twentieth day we are considering that 'Oldenburg' has lost 670 points while its enemy, Hesse-Hanau, has lost but 420. According to our dictum, then, both would receive replacements at the lesser figure, that is, 420 points. However, reviewing the situation, we see that during the twenty days two of Hesse-Hanau's cities and one of its towns had been in enemy occupation for more than the prescribed eight days. This means that a total of 12% (2 at 5% and 1 at 2%) must be denied to this power and so, instead of the full 420 points of replacements a loss of 12% – or 50 points in round figures – has to be endured, the total therefore being reduced to 370 from 420. In effect, all this means that while the infliction of battle casualties is naturally the most important factor in our campaign, nevertheless, as it was in the 18th Century, the occupation of enemy territory and the consequent deprivation of the resources from that area has an important bearing upon military operations. All this does entail a certain amount of book-keeping – maintaining records of casualties, assessing fatalities and wounded, and noting the time towns and cities are occupied.

Many additional points which could be advantageous in waging a campaign, will occur to the participants as they progress. Indeed it is wholly impossible to undertake such an enterprise without problems presenting themselves to the players. One which might profitably be mentioned in conclusion is the possibly inevitable temptation for generally the less experienced and, dare I say it, the less historically orientated player, to gather all his troops together in a mass, thus unrealistically abandoning lines of communication and at the same time the defence of vital areas of his own country and rush madly forward in an attempt to 'seek and destroy'. There are even methods by which this can be countered. It is possible, for instance, to lay down limitations on the time that a certain force can be maintained when concentrated in one body – obviously the problem of supply would ensure rapid dispersal over a wider area than its point of assembly. Certain units of an army can be raised for home service only, cities for example, having their own municipal guard regiments, which would not be permitted to serve away from home. In a slightly larger context, local defence battalions can be organised – similar to the European frontier or *Grenze* battalions – to operate only within national borders. They might be of less fighting value than regular line regiments, but would perform a useful function in defence.

These then are the basics of wargame campaigning.

15
Something about Colour

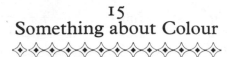

One of the most pleasant feelings a wargamer can experience, after having deployed a substantial army on his table, is to stand back and contemplate the splendour of his massed soldiery, and to regard their variegated uniforms, colours and standards. Certainly the satisfaction of being able to field miniature troops whose appearance is something of which their owner can be proud, is a most understandable one. A large part of this feeling – a much more considerable portion than may ordinarily be admitted by many enthusiasts – is the simple and unequivocal delight to be obtained in moving about on a wargames table, figures which are both colourfully and, within the historical framework of their period, accurately painted. This is one reason, of course, why the wargamer will tend to choose a period of history in which the troops of the time were clad in bright and impressive uniforms. In this regard, none is more splendid than that of the battle we have studied – the middle years of the 18th Century.

There can be no question but that a battle in this

epoch was a most staggering spectacle from the point of view of colour if not from that of humanitarianism. The sight of great masses of blue, red or white uniformed men marching and counter-marching in stately and impressive manoeuvres must have been quite breathtaking. It is part of the charisma of wargaming that such sights in miniature can readily be created to delight the aesthetic senses of players and spectators alike. In our period we are fortunate that even by adhering rigidly to contemporary regulations governing military costume and equipment we can nevertheless have troops clad in almost every colour of the rainbow. Even allowing for the fact that the dyes of a couple of centuries ago did not produce such vivid colours as those in use today, the results were still striking in the extreme.

Apart from the simple colours in general use, to my mind the actual design of the uniforms was impressive, but in this connection I hasten to add that, where uniforms are concerned, it is very largely a matter for personal taste, one person being committed to the uniform types of the Napoleonic period, for example, while another may opt unhesitatingly for the sartorial ebullience of the 17th Century. For myself, I have no reluctance in my choice, which is for the great years of the 18th Century, when both the colours and the cut of the uniforms presented a most pleasing effect. That these uniforms were very far from being practical and left much to be desired from the point of view of the wearer's comfort is neither here nor there – it is with the effect upon the beholder that we are concerned.

Considering infantry first, if I may, generally speaking we find that the foot soldier wore a long and capacious coat, reaching almost to the knee and covering a waistcoat itself fairly lengthy, and covered by cross belts supporting small sword and ammunition pouch. In normal cases the outfit was completed by a three-cornered hat, breeches and gaiters buttoned on the outside of the leg and reaching as high as mid-thigh. About the middle of the century the coat, which had formerly been almost always worn open in front was beginning to be buttoned up and to be held in place by a waistbelt. The full skirts of the coat were also increasingly buttoned back, giving increased freedom for leg movement.

At this time there was no question of using dark or neutral colours for uniforms with the aim of providing a less obvious target, at least not for infantry of the line, the idea as yet having been tentatively mooted only for light infantry. Prussian *jäger* for instance are usually to be found wearing dark green, but even formations who might have been expected to clothe themselves in colours with the ability to merge with the surroundings, the better to carry out their special tasks, were just as brightly attired as any line infantry, as we shall presently see in the case of our friends, the Arquebussiers de Grassin.

All in all, though, each national army had its basic uniform colour for infantry. Every schoolboy knows that the British hue was red, this being not a true scarlet but something in the nature of a brick-red, although it was bright enough. Since the Battle of Fontenoy has been our theme, it might be opportune to point out that the basic uniform colour for French infantry was officially 'white', but this is something of a misnomer, for at the time with which we are concerned the shade was rather darker than a true white, more of a definite 'off white' or even a very light grey.

Prussian infantry of the line traditionally wore dark blue, and their Russian equivalents dark green. This is a very general statement, though, for to all these I have mentioned there were several exceptions, not least in the French army, where large numbers of regiments, customarily the non-native French ones, had coats of colours other than the white already mentioned. Many such units were in the service of the Kings of France, Swiss and Irish predominating, together with Germans and other nationalities. A Royal Scots regiment was in French service for many years, and after the 'Forty five' several others appeared in the army lists of France. Like the British line, Swiss and Irish regiments in Saxe's army wore red coats, and some of the others were clad in blue, but all – and this applies to infantry of every nationality – were identified as units through variations of what was called the facing colour, this also being used for collars and cuffs, while sometimes the long waistcoat was also of the distinctive colour. Buttons, too, were a source of difference between regiments, either through the material of their manufacture – brass or pewter – or their arrangement on cuffs and pocket flaps. Frequently, in addition, one finds the cuffs and the breast of the uniform coat ornamented with 'loops' of lace, usually white, particularly in the British Army, although the white was from time to time interwoven with lines of one or more other colours. The number and shape of the 'loops' also differed in many cases between regiments.

In most infantry regiments was to be found a company of grenadiers who stood out most conspicuously from their fellows. Originally, in the latter half of the 17th Century a small party of men from each battalion of infantry had been selected to throw the primitive grenades of the period, and as these were both heavy and clumsy, only the biggest and most powerful men were selected for this duty. The arm action required by the grenadier when hurtling his missile was such that the broad-brimmed tricorne – the three cornered hat – was a considerable hindrance. Because of this another article of headgear was adopted, the 'mitre cap', a tall, pointed cap not unlike, as the name implies, that of a bishop. It was later ornamented with fur and over the years gradually developed into the Foot Guards' bearskin of the present day. With the turn of the century the use of the grenade was discontinued, but the grenadiers were maintained, developing into the 'crack' company of the regiment, taking station on the right flank and having the best and biggest men in their ranks. The distinctive mitre cap was also long retained in one form or another. The cap, by the way, could be an extremely elaborate affair, with a great deal of embroidery, badges and crests ornamenting its front, especially in the British Army.

Equally as diverse were the uniforms worn by the various light infantry units now appearing – in the middle of the 18th Century, of course – in many armies on the continent. Highly placed individuals and generals charged with the raising of such units vied apparently with each other in equipping and uniforming their regiments in the most colourful and even bizarre manner. If we take those already known to us, the Arquebussiers de Grassin, as an example, we see at once just what sort of appearance was enjoyed by one of these semi-regular units. The Grassins wore a long, full coat of a sort of royal blue, edged, strangely enough, with white fur on front, lapels and cuffs. The waistcoat was red, ornamented with yellow braiding, and blue breeches and long black gaiters made up the remainder of this somewhat spectacular garb, the whole being surmounted by a headdress of the type known as the *mirliton*, a blunt-ended cone with a dependent cloth streamer which could be either worn loose or wrapped round the actual headgear. This was scarlet, topped with a white plume. Nor were the Arquebussiers more outstanding than others of their ilk, such corps as the Fusiliers de la Morlière – chocolate brown and red – and the Chasseurs de Fischer – green and red – being but two of a number of equally dazzling units. British units were rather dull in comparison with such gaudy finery, wearing the universal dull red, although the dark tartan of the Black Watch made them conspicuous in the general run of regiments.

It goes without saying that the cavalry of the time, always a traditionally colourful arm, were similarly splendid, and in some cases provided even greater variety than did their dismounted brethren. In the case of these mounted troops there was no specially distinctive colour for the various armies, no one shade being really dominant. Household Cavalry – such as the Maison du Roi – seem to have favoured red, although blue did appear, and some regiments wore bright steel breastplates – cuirasses. In the British Army were to be found

Horse Grenadiers who, like their infantry counterparts, wore the high mitre cap, and all cavalrymen rode horses with highly ornamented saddle cloths and pistol holsters, emblazoned with intricate coats of arms and crests. Appearing in some continental armies we find a new type of light cavalry – at this time largely in the south east of Europe – these being hussars, originally from Hungary. They wore fur hats and an additional short jacket – the pelisse – sometimes slung over the left shoulder. The dress of such troops reflected their outlandish origins.

One can readily see that a lively pleasure may be had from deploying an army as colourful as we have indicated. To the uniforms themselves may be added the numerous standards and colours which were customary in the armies of our period. Each British battalion had two, the King's and Regimental Colours, and the French did not lag behind, the standard for most native French regiments being basically a white cross (of the style we call St. George's) with the four quarters in various colours, and sometimes embroidered with sun emblems, *fleurs de lys* and the like.

So we can see that the aesthetic requirement which is part of the wargaming hobby is more than adequately catered for by our 18th Century armies. Nor need it be feared that the painting of the considerable number of figures necessary for a large scale wargame will be a tedious and prolonged business. Without a doubt, whatever effort is called for is more than compensated for by the satisfaction of seeing one's miniature recruits grow in numbers and in sartorial perfection as one's painting skill improves. With the quality of figures provided by manufacturers today, painting has become a relatively easy matter, and as long as one does not try to cope with too many at once, it will be found to be a real joy to sit down and produce an impressive looking line of military soldiery, a regiment of British Guards, a company of Fusiliers de la Montagne, or a squadron of the Gendarmerie du Roi. They, and their numerous fellows, are well worth the trouble.

Appendix 1
Bibliography

❖ ❖-❖-❖-❖ ❖-❖

For convenience this section has been divided into two parts, the first dealing with books devoted to wargaming as a hobby, the second with the most easily accessible historical sources enabling one to study the military art of the time.

I have decided to include in the former, not only volumes directly concerned with wargaming in the 18th Century, but general works as well as more specialised ones relating to other periods, the aim being to provide readers who might not necessarily concern themselves with horse and musket warfare with the background for setting up wargames in other epochs they might find more to their liking.

The number of historical works quoted in Section Two is strictly limited. A vast number of histories and treatises exist dealing with every facet of the subject, and should the reader wish to delve further it will be for him an easy matter to seek information in the bibliographies of those volumes referred to below.

Section One
Advanced Wargames, D. F. Featherstone (1969).
Air Wargames, D. F. Featherstone (1967).
Battle! Practical Wargaming, Charles Grant (1970).
Battles With Model Soldiers, D. F. Featherstone (1970).
Charge!, Brigadier Peter Young & Lt. Colonel J. Lawford (1967).
Discovering Wargames, John Tunstill (1969).
Naval Wargames, D. F. Featherstone (1966).
Napoleonic Wargaming, Charles Grant (1974).
Solo Wargames, D. F. Featherstone (1972).
The Ancient Wargame, Charles Grant (1974).
The Wargame, Charles Grant (1971).
Wargames, D. F. Featherstone (1962).
Wargames in Miniature, J. Morschauser (1963).
Wargames Campaigns, D. F. Featherstone (1970).
Wargames Through The Ages, Vol. I, D. F. Featherstone (1972).

Section Two

C. T. Atkinson: *History of Germany 1715–1815* (1908).
H. L. Blackmore: *British Military Firearms 1650–1850* (1961).
L. Cooper: *British Regular Cavalry 1644–1914* (1965).
G. T. Denison: *History of Cavalry* (1877).
C. Duffy: *The Wild Goose and the Eagle* (1964).
J. F. C. Fuller: *British Light Infantry in the Eighteenth Century* (1925).
C. James: *New and Enlarged Military Dictionary* (1810).
L. Kennett: *The French Armies in the Seven Years War* (1967).
E. M. Lloyd: *A Review of the History of Infantry* (1908).
J. Lunt: *Scarlet Lancer* (1964).
J. Muller: *A Treatise of Artillery* (1768).
R. Savory: *His Britannic Majesty's Army in Germany during the Seven Years War* (1966).
R. E. Scouller: *The Armies of Queen Anne.*
F. H. B. Skrine: *Fontenoy and Great Britain's Share in the War of the Austrian Succession* (1906).
J. M. White: *Marshal of France : the Life and Times of Maurice, Comte de Saxe* (1962).
R. Whitworth: *Field Marshal Lord Ligonier.*

Appendix 2
Availability of Wargame Figures

❖◆❖◆❖◆❖◆❖◆❖◆❖◆❖◆❖◆❖

At no time has the wargamer been as fortunate in the sheer number of available figures as he is today, with new firms constantly appearing and with quite enormous increases to the already existing lines. The extremely fine quality of some of these newer products never ceases to astonish, particularly when one thinks of the pretty primitive models the 'old timer' had to employ in his wargames, and many of these, when painted with care and a modicum of skill, will stand comparison with much larger craftsman-designed types.

Those listed below are, admittedly, the best known ones, and by the time these words appear in print the list may well be out-of-date, with new manufacturers being in production. Three different sizes of figure are mentioned, the 15 mm., the 25 mm., and the 30 mm. The 20 mm. is so frequently bracketed with the 25 mm., and the sizes of the two species are so frequently nearly identical, that for convenience the 20 mm. has been included with his slightly larger brother.

Airfix Ltd. These are the figures, in plastic, whose appearance revolutionised the model soldier market. Their size, it is admitted, varies considerably, but they can, at a stretch, be described as 25 mm., although many are much less than this.

Garrison Figures (Greenwood and Ball Ltd). Originally produced 20 mm. models, but now concentrate on a substantial 25 mm. size. For some time specialised in 'ancient' types, but have expanded very largely into Napoleonic and 18th Century periods.

Hinchliffe Miniatures. This is a very large range of 25 mm. figures, largely 'ancient' and Napoleonic, but English Civil War and Colonial figures are also in the firm's list. Hinchliffe model guns, in 20 mm., 25 mm., and 30 mm sizes are quite definitely the best on the market at present.

Hinton Hunt Figures. A considerable range of 20 mm. figures, of a very wide variety of periods, especially mediaeval and Napoleonic.

Lamming Miniatures. 25 mm. figures in a good variety of types, particularly Napoleonic and 'ancient'.

Miniature Figurines. This firm has a huge list of figures in 15 mm., 25 mm., and 30 mm. Virtually every period is covered in very considerable numbers and new ones are constantly appearing.

Phoenix Model Developments Ltd. Models in the 20 mm., 25 mm., and 30 mm. sizes. Very well detailed figures, including early 18th Century and English Civil War types.

Rose Miniatures. 20 mm. figures have been produced by this firm for some time, but lately a new series of 30 mm. types have been brought out, with Napoleonic Wars and Colonial Wars being included.

Spencer Smith Figures. Apart from Airfix, the only firm mentioned which produces plastics, these being in 30 mm. Not as detailed as metal models, naturally, they are nevertheless extremely inexpensive and excellent for the wargamer desirous of building up large armies. Concentrates on Napoleonics and late 18th Century soldiers.

Tradition Figures. A relative newcomer to the wargame figure scene, this firm has long been associated with the famous Charles Stadden, who is also one of the craftsmen designing this new 25 mm. range. A large number of Napoleonic types are available, and many 18th Century as well, while the American Civil War and the Franco Prussian War both figure among their products.

Warrior Miniatures. In both 25 mm. and 30 mm. sizes, this firm produces a considerable variety of figures in almost all popular periods.

Willie Figures. 30 mm. figures of very high quality and in the principal periods, Napoleonic, 18th Century and Colonial especially.

Addresses for these firms have not been given, as most intending purchasers will endeavour, I feel, to seek out their products at their nearest hobby shop, where they will have the added pleasure of examining them before acquisition. The average shop carries at least two firms' products in my experience.

Index